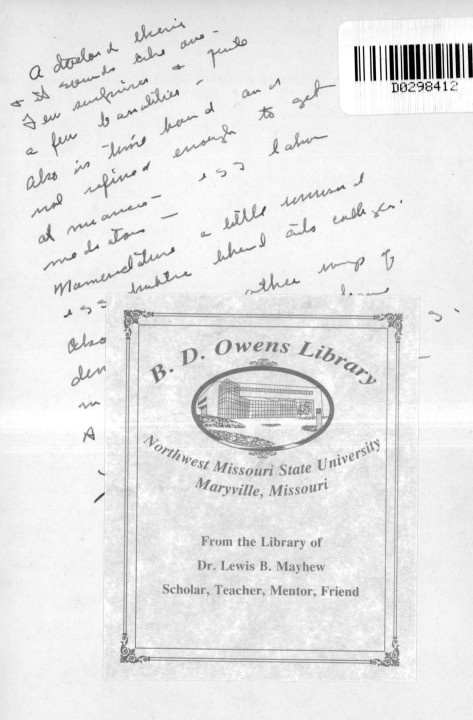

*Profiles of
American College Presidents*

Profiles of
American College Presidents

by
Michael R. Ferrari

with a foreword by
W. Lloyd Warner

1970
MSU BUSINESS STUDIES

Division of Research
Graduate School of Business Administration
Michigan State University
East Lansing, Michigan

To Janice

Contents

List of Tables

Appendix Tables

Foreword

From the days of the early Republic to the present time the opinions and activities of college presidents have interested and often strongly influenced Americans. Their own publications on the state of the nation, the world, and on higher education, as well as the books and articles written about them, frequently had large audiences. In the early years of the nineteenth century a massive report on the culture of New England and New York by Timothy Dwight, a one-time president of Yale, gave Americans the benefit of his lofty judgments about social conditions, the manners and morals of that part of the country. The books and articles by Charles Eliot and A. Lawrence Lowell of Harvard, of Andrew White of Cornell, Nicholas Murray Butler at Columbia, William Rainey Harper of the University of Chicago and David Starr Jordan of Stanford in the last century and the first decades of this one were read by many Americans, just as have the writings of Clark Kerr and other presidents of contemporary times. Some who read their publications were interested in their knowledge, more in their opinions, and all who read were interested in their personal lives and in finding out inside information about their presidencies. Biographies and autobiographies of prominent presidents of colleges and universities are eagerly sought by publishers. The isolated campuses and ivory towers once cherished and protected by their cloistered inhabitants have long since been abandoned. Today they are subjects only of historical reconstruction. The involvement of modern colleges and universities with advancing learning, developing pure science, applying academic research to scientific technology and helping solve individual and social problems have pulled institutions of higher learning, their presidents, their professors and their students into the complex affairs of industry, government, and the small and large activities of all segments of American life. Moreover, the present social revolution that brings conflict everywhere to university affairs, the frictions felt in the rapidly changing roles of presidents, professors, students and trustees, the hot disagreements about what should be the proper course of higher education, and the constant attention, and sometimes meddling, of the mass media in university affairs now immediately draws everyone, university trained or not, into the public drama of conflict. This adds greatly to the problem of running a university.

The university president is the man in the middle of all this hell-raising. While he tries to raise badly needed dollars to finance his institution, struggles to maintain and advance his university, while he strives to keep abreast of new developments in learning and help recruit new personnel to strengthen weak departments, he must try vainly to curb violence to protect the age-old learning and teaching activities of any good institution of higher learning. Meanwhile, students, sometimes joined by substantial numbers of the faculty, protest violently, alumni complain, and trustees issue stern warnings. For many, the college president has "a hell of a job"; Who would want it? What kind of people and what kind of men and women occupy this difficult position? Why are they there? What are their origins and backgrounds? What kinds of careers have led to their accepting election to college presidencies? Do they themselves perceive their jobs as difficult and beyond the demands they can fulfill in administering the affairs of their institutions? Do they themselves see their jobs as being in a lower circle of an inferno?

Until very recently, little was known systematically about academic presidents and about the career lines of this important occupational elite in American society. The present volume on the careers and perceptions of university and college presidents tells us much about them. It is an excellent product of extensive research conducted by the author, Dr. Michael R. Ferrari, who provides the answers to these and many other questions about the lives, careers, and opinions of 760 university and college presidents. Dr. Ferrari's excellent volume, *Profiles of American College Presidents,* is a revision of his doctoral dissertation written in 1968 at Michigan State University and it is an important contribution to our understanding of the careers of these men. It is also a valuable contribution to our knowledge about occupational mobility in America and a solid addition to what we know about American society. When the author

compares the facts about the careers of college presidents with those
of other elites in America—such as those of business, corporations
and government—we learn immediately in what ways the college
presidents' lives are like or not like those of the other occupants of
high position.

The family origins of the men and women who are now college and
university presidents range all the way from the bottom to the top of
our occupational structure and class system, from men whose
fathers were unskilled workers at the bottom, to those at the top
whose fathers were big businessmen or in the higher professions.
This volume tells us, however, that more presidents came from
homes at the higher levels; we learn that a significant percentage of
these presidents came up the long route to the top and were not born
to high position; about one-fourth of them had fathers who were
workers, 18 per cent were blue collar, and 5 per cent, white collar.
This study demonstrates that in this area, as in other important
areas of American life, the road to the top is open and can be tra-
versed all the way by men and women of talent, ability, and the
necessary training.

Such an important general conclusion must raise questions in the
reader's mind about the representativeness and the reliability of the
evidence on which it is founded. The 760 men and women in this
study were carefully drawn from all types of American colleges and
universities, Catholic, Protestant, public and private. Both Negro
and white institutions were included, large and small institutions of
higher learning that grant only A.B.s and those with established
graduate schools that grant a variety of advanced degrees. The institutions here are a representative sample of colleges and universities
of the United States and their presidents are representative of the
men and women who occupy these high positions.

These men come from all over America, from every section of the
country and from every type of community—small town, rural area,
big city and metropolis. Slightly over one-fourth came from New
England and the Middle Atlantic regions, about 30 per cent more
from the Deep South and western southern states, another 37 per
cent from the Northern Central States and under 10 per cent from
the Mountain and Pacific States.

One constantly reads in the public press about the new "boy
wonders," the young and younger men who occupy the presidents'
chairs. Just how old are these men? How do their ages compare with

those of presidents of corporations and the heads of great government agencies? As a matter of hard fact, established by the results
of Ferrari's research, we learn here that the differences of average
age of these elites, academic, corporate and government, are very
small. The average age of corporate leaders was fifty-four, government men, forty-nine, and academic presidents, fifty-three.

An opinion about them I have shared with many professors and
others interested in academic affairs, one which was not dissipated
by the seeming ineptitudes of some college presidents in recent
moments of conflict, crisis, campus riots, and major disruptions, was
that their likely backgrounds were research labs, scholarly hideouts
or protected lecture halls which did not give them tough training
necessary for their present posts. How many presidents have previous administrative training for their present posts that would be
likely to give them the equipment to make the hard, on-the-line decisions that keep universities doing the job of maintaining necessary relations between learners and teachers, and between
community and university? From Ferrari's research, my earlier
belief appears biased and not founded on solid fact: three-fourths
of these men and women had previous experience at lower levels of
leadership in the academic hierarchy; 7 per cent were presidents
of other universities where they had had earlier seasoning, and
most of the rest had been in positions of authority in corporations,
the military, government or other organizations. The presidents are
not men whose minds are absent in abstractions of professional
thought—the so-called absent-minded professors—and they are not
inexperienced with the practical task of managing others to accomplish common educational purposes. Most have had solid preparation for the posts they now occupy.

Responses by them to inquiries about how they feel about their
jobs, how they perceive their jobs, and why they are in them demon-
strate that most have a strong sense of public service and a dedica-
tion to the ideals of higher education and teaching, that they have
superior standards about what educated men should know and
about the well being of the world in which we live. These responses
about the role of the president of a university often appear deeply
felt, not merely pious rhetoric, given publicly by a public figure.
Many of the responses, in spirit and values, are like the following:

> *"I have a deep conviction that I have a responsibility to other*

*men for service. This—with a love for young people—makes
the academic setting attractive. The opportunity to further the
cause was made available in administration."*

*"Though it sounds immodest, I have a sense of noblesse oblige
[from] my family which had a tradition of civic leadership."*

Although these men and women take themselves seriously and
their jobs as college and university presidents very seriously, many
reveal a sense of humor—sometimes ironic and sometimes self-
applied. They have implicit feelings about their own limitations that
help free them from stuffiness and overevaluation of their own persons and talents. Some may be egotists but few, if any, are egocen-
trics. All seem to live in the very real present as it now moves to the
ever demanding future. Given the quandaries of solving present
conflicts, given their being targets of juvenile and sometimes irrational attacks, it might be supposed that they would betray signs of
unhappiness, of being in a weak position, of thinking their jobs were
too much for any man and impossible to handle.

While all appear constantly aware of the limitations of their positions and many speak of drawbacks, none feels his job is too difficult and all feel that there are many real satisfactions from being
where they are. Most, if not all, like their job and feel sufficiently
equipped to respond to its pressing demands. They all believe they
have the necessary personal and professional equipment and talent
to perform more than adequately.

As such they are successful men and women who occupy a powerful and prestigeful elite position, who, as the elites of other segments
of American life, government and business among them, have
advanced to the top of their profession.

Dr. Ferrari's fine volume on their careers contributes to our
understanding of upward mobility of an academic elite, adds solid
knowledge to what we know about social stratification, and provides
social science with an excellent study of a significant segment of
contemporary America.

W. Lloyd Warner
University Professor Emeritus
Michigan State University

Acknowledgments

This research has benefitted from the assistance and support of a number of people. Without their valuable contributions the study most certainly could not have been conducted. The study was completed while I was at Michigan State University, and special gratitude is extended to the M.S.U. faculty members who contributed to various aspects of the research design, study, and writing. Invaluable criticism, recommendations, and encouragement have been given by: Professor W. Lloyd Warner, University Professor of Social Research; Dr. Dalton McFarland, Professor and Chairman of the Management Department; Dr. Edward Blackman, Professor of Education; and Dr. Stanley Stark, Professor of Management.

In particular, the study is greatly indebted to the late Professor Warner, who provided the basic theoretical framework and methodology adapted to the present research. The influence of his extensive research of occupational mobility among elites in this society is surely reflected in the study of American college and university presidents. The academic president research has also benefitted from a Ford Foundation doctoral fellowship grant.

Special thanks are extended to three friends and colleagues who offered suggestions on various phases of the research and assisted in the coding of questionnaires: Mrs. Carolyn McManaman, Mr. Morey Villareal, and Miss Priscilla Overman. Also, Mrs. Mary Lu Hough of the Division of Research at Michigan State University, who assisted greatly in editing the final manuscript.

Finally, I owe a very special gratitude to my wife, Janice, who provided continuous encouragement and patience throughout the project.

1

Introduction

The diversity of American colleges and universities is a prevalent theme in scholarly and professional publications as well as in the mass media. These institutions have been shown to be diverse in philosophy, objectives, structure, size, complexity, form of control, and financial aspects. Each institution, whether public or private, large or small, Ivy-League or teachers college, faces the difficult task of staffing its top administrative positions with individuals capable of providing effective educational leadership within the contemporary college climate. Controversial issues in governmental and community relations, institutional autonomy, and faculty-student demands of increased roles in significant areas of decision making, such as curriculum, experimental programs, policy formulation, and general governance of the institution are only a few of the more pressing problems that have become associated with academia.

Although much has already been written and said about the administrative, educational, and financial problems facing the nation's colleges and universities, only recently has attention from multifarious sources focused so decisively on those persons charged with the fundamental responsibility of resolving these problems, that is, the college and university presidents.

A careful review of the literature on academic presidents shows that we know relatively little in any systematic sense about the men and women who head the nation's institutions of higher education. What is known about college presidents regarding their career patterns, roles, personalities, and socioeconomic characteristics has come primarily from the personal essays, speeches, and memoirs of former presidents. These writings have given rich insights into elements of the academic presidency, but they are generally quite limited in perspective or are lacking in knowledge of a factual-empirical nature. Although there have been empirical investigations of the careers of leaders in the federal government and American big business, few studies with any degree of scientific sophistication have been directed toward giving greater understanding of the careers of chief administrators in higher education.

The research reported in this book attempts to provide not only a more systematic and accurate career profile of academic presidents, but to give additional insights into occupational mobility of this elite in American society. It presents the findings of research on the careers of 760 college and university presidents. Men and women who head public, Catholic, Protestant-related, and independent, four-year institutions are among the educational leaders studied.

Purposes of the Study

The primary purpose of the study was to investigate the social origins, professional training, and career patterns of the presidents of the accredited, four-year liberal arts colleges and accredited universities in the United States. The research was intended to produce: (1) an accurate analysis of the career patterns, occupational mobility, and social-personal characteristics of these leaders; (2) cross-comparisons of these presidents on the basis of public and types of private institutions; and (3) intensive comparisons of the careers of academic presidents with the careers of business and government executives.

The study examines a number of specific questions that support the primary purpose. Who are the presidents of American colleges and universities? How did they get to these positions? How long did it take to get there? What seem to be the techniques and avenues of career mobility in higher educational administration? Are persons with certain professional and social backgrounds found in one kind of institution rather than another? What are the ages of these men and what do we know about their families? What were the occupational backgrounds of their fathers, paternal grandfathers, maternal grandfathers, and wives' fathers? What were the educational backgrounds of their parents? Where were the presidents and their wives, parents, and grandparents born?

Where were the presidents educated and what were their fields of interest? Why did these persons choose the ultimate careers and positions they did, especially college and university administration? What other career alternatives were seriously considered and why were the alternatives rejected? Are there pronounced differences between and among the careers of academic presidents themselves and with the careers of business and government executives?

Theoretical Framework

The study was conceived to fall within the same theoretical and methodological framework which brought forth research on vertical occupational mobility among other specific elites in American society. W. Lloyd Warner and James Abegglen developed and put into operation an approach to the scientific inquiry of the business elite; their theories on occupation and family structure in this society serve as the fundamental underpinnings of the study of academic presidents.

A brief review of the major theoretical contributions stated by Warner and Abegglen provides a perspective that will permit critical evaluation of the types of questions raised and the findings obtained.[1] Pivotal concepts in the theory of occupational mobility are *occupational succession* and the *theory of family structure*. Occupational succession refers to

the ordered process by which individuals succeed each other in occupations. The study of occupational succession, therefore, consists of examining the circulation and movement of personnel through positions, and of determining the regularities and uniformities which have to do with entering, hold-

1. Material reviewed in this section has been taken from W. Lloyd Warner and James C. Abegglen, *Occupational Mobility* (Minneapolis: University of Minnesota Press, 1955), pp. 4–36.

ing, and leaving a given status. . . . More particularly, this investigation of occupational succession is concerned with how this society orders and determines which men, through the changing generations of individuals, shall occupy certain occupational statuses.[2]

The notion of family structure is interrelated with occupational succession as it encompasses the process that ". . . men are born to fathers who are at given occupational levels, they grow to maturity, learn and follow a particular profession in life, marry, sire sons who are reared to maturity and work at their own trades or professions."[3] Warner and Abegglen found that the movement or lack of movement among occupations can be measured by the use of the birth cycle or the unit of time between an individual's own birth and the birth of his child. The occupational movement of fathers and sons can be identified and measured by noting the particular occupational status held by each and the amount of occupational movement between the generations. When such a movement is combined with the age of the particular leader when he achieved his present position, the velocity of movement as well as the direction and amount can be determined.

In addition, it is possible to interrelate the occupations of different generations through studying the occupation of the wife's father. A study of the wives' social origins helps determine whether: (1) leaders moved into a particular occupational level, whether it be business, government, or higher education, by marriage and possibly acquired it without earning it; (2) leaders achieved elite positions and then married a woman at the newly acquired rank; or (3) leaders married either at their level of origin or someone along the way to high position. It is for these reasons that Warner and Abegglen and also the research reported on in this book examine the occupation of the wife's father.

It has long been recognized that in American society, occupation, marriage, and descent are interwoven into what has been called a single "status-giving system" and such a phenomenon indicates whether the social system is open, allowing vertical status movement, or closed, such as a caste system, or somewhere between. For the earlier studies based on this theory, two major types of persons were found at the elite levels: the birth elite (those born into the

2. Ibid., p. 4.
3. Ibid.

particular status level) and the mobile elite (those often born into lower levels who achieved the high positions by movement into it). These ideas lead to the following questions: Were academic presidents born to high educational positions, based upon their fathers' occupations, or if extended another generation back, to the grandfathers' occupations? Did they move into their present positions from other—lower, higher, lateral—occupational levels? Did they marry at the same level, above or below in terms of occupational status?

It must be mentioned that Warner and Abegglen were concerned about whether American society was more or less open in 1952 (when the big business leader study was conducted) than from an earlier study by Taussig and Joslyn in 1928.[4] The existence of the earlier study gave a valuable time interval to assess the dynamics of societal fluidity that strengthened the theoretical and methodological base of occupational succession. In addition, it permitted many insights for nearly a century in American business leadership. There is no earlier, comparable base-line study for the research on the careers of academic presidents that will yield similar comparisons. However, it is assumed that the results of this study give further implications for the existing fluidity in this society when seen through another occupational hierarchy.

Interrelated propositions dovetailing with the general notion of occupational succession deal with other features related to the mobility of elites. It was assumed and later substantiated by Warner and Abegglen that the size of a man's birthplace and the region in which he was born (that is, his geographical origins) play a part in occupational mobility. In addition, it was found that the degree of spatial mobility and circulation of these men in the course of their careers was important; the corollary that "men who are mobile through social space are also mobile through geographic space" found empirical support. Based upon such general propositions, this study asked whether academic presidents are representative of certain regions and communities rather than others. Have they moved physically from one place to another and if so, what was the nature of the movement?

The theory of occupational mobility among elites holds that the amount and kind of education one receives is critically related to

4. F. W. Taussig and C. S. Joslyn, *American Business Leaders* (New York: The Macmillan Company, 1932).

successful mobility. Obviously, college and university presidents provide leadership within educational institutions and can be easily assumed to be very well-educated. It is pertinent to determine whether a particular kind of education at particular institutions is seemingly related to their mobility and how their entrance into education might be linked to social origins.

Mobility as a concept is also important when considering if these men moved up an educational hierarchy or if they had prior positions outside the field of education, for example, in business, government, farming, or other occupations. This idea has relevance in exploring the whole notion of career patterns as it relates to a theory of occupational succession. That is, how did the presidents move within their own careers? How long did it take to move from the first full-time position to the presidency? What career routes were formed along the way by such movement?

This study must be viewed as an intensive investigation of occupational mobility into higher educational administrative leadership. It is assumed that mobility into the academic administrative elite is a function of more general social factors. Therefore, the results of the study may be related to occupational mobility in the other occupational hierarchies. It should be kept in mind that the research does not deal with the specific problem of social class mobility, although it has been recognized as being tied to occupational mobility.

In short, selected key features of the theory developed and tested by Warner and Abegglen have been adapted to the study of academic presidents in a way that will: (1) shed light on the presidents as an occupational elite themselves; (2) permit comparisons with other elite groups; and (3) contribute to the theory of occupational mobility in the ever-changing, emerging social system of American society.

2

Historical Development

Most writings of the social origins, educational backgrounds, personal qualities, and career patterns of academic presidents, as well as the general development of the academic presidency, have been prepared mainly by college presidents in the form of memoirs, speeches, essays, and biographies. These publications offer a number of insights into the careers, lives, and roles of these higher educational administrators. Complementing such writings are a few recent accounts that provide broader and more systematic investigations of various aspects of the role, selection process, and careers of selected groups of college presidents.

In Colonial College Days

From the founding of Harvard College in 1636 to the eve of the American Revolution, the colonies brought forth a total of nine colleges, largely patterned after England's Oxford and Cambridge.[1]

1. Harvard was joined by William and Mary in 1693, Yale in 1701, Pennsylvania in 1740, Princeton in 1746, Columbia in 1754, Brown in 1764, Rutgers in 1766, and Dartmouth in 1769.

The general image of the colonial college was a small, religious-oriented institution shaped by and intended to serve the more aristocratic elements of colonial society.[2] It has been estimated that in 1776 there were only 3,000 living graduates of the American colleges.[3]

The position and title of the American college president began with Henry Dunster at Harvard in 1640.[4] Other titles had their beginnings in the colonial colleges as well, for example, Yale had a *rector* for nearly fifty years and Penn had a *provost.* The title *chancellor* was adopted later by a number of private institutions and is still widely used to identify a college or university's chief administrative officer.[5]

The growth of the college presidency was spurred by two main factors, according to Ralph Prator, who wrote:

In colonial times, the control of colleges increasingly fell to a board of men chosen from outside the professorate, an idea taken from the Scots. It meant, however, that the board was forced to rely heavily on the president to assume executive-type responsibilities. The board's authority came to be essentially centered in the presidential office; and

Also in colonial times, the teaching staff members were seldom permanent and had little professional cohesiveness. Often, the president was one of few permanent members of a college staff. The only secure and sustained professional office in American collegiate education was that of the college president himself.[6]

The office of the president is uniquely American, even though it was modeled on English precedents, according to George P. Schmidt, who maintains that

the president was a more important figure than the presidents or principals of the colleges of Oxford and Cambridge, who though their powers were expanding, were primarily the senior fellows; and his functions were much

---

2. Frederick Rudolph, *The American College and University: A History* (New York: Vintage Books, 1965), p. 18.
3. Ibid., p. 22.
4. Charles F. Thwing, *The College President* (New York: The MacMillan Company, 1926), pp. 1–2.
5. For a more detailed discussion of the European origins of the titles, see Charles F. Thwing, Ibid., pp. 4–9.
6. Ralph Prator, *The College President* (Washington, D.C.: The Center for Applied Research in Education, Inc., 1963), p. 9.

broader and more varied than those of the rectors and chancellors of the large European universities.[7]

Schmidt goes on to say that ". . . the most important individual in the early college was the president. He was the leader of a comparatively uncomplicated institution." In fact, many early colleges were often portrayed as "lengthened shadows of the president."[8]

The colonial college president has been pictured in the literature as rather autocratic and often despotic in his leadership style, and as patriarch as well as chief administrator in his purpose. The most essential qualification for the early president included: (1) he must be a clergyman, (2) he must be an excellent speaker, and (3) he must be able to raise money and direct the administration of the college.[9] Schmidt found that there was not a single lay president in the entire colonial period—they were all ordained ministers.[10] Later writings have indicated that only a few non-clergymen were selected for the academic presidency well into the nineteenth century.

The early president was indeed more concerned with teaching—he himself taught subjects usually oriented to Christianity—rather than research. With a relatively youthful college population, he was also more involved in the development of a student's character.[11]

Growth and Changes

The stable, quiet, passive era of the colonial college gave way to the exciting and dynamic social, economic, and political changes in America following the Revolutionary War. The climate of America, which included the cultivating of a national pride and a more critical appraisal of how valuable a staid group of "gentlemen-scholars" would be in creating cities out of the wilderness, forced reform and reaction to the traditional, classical college curriculum. In 1780 there were only nine colleges, but at the outbreak of the Civil War

7. George P. Schmidt, *The Liberal Arts College* (New Brunswick: Rutgers University Press, 1957), pp. 103–4.
8. Ibid., p. 103.
9. Prator, *The College President*, p. 6.
10. Ibid.
11. Ibid., p. 7.

the country had a total of 182 colleges—while over 400 institutions opened and failed during this period.[12]

In the last half of the nineteenth century there were extraordinary changes that affected the presidency and higher education. The founding of Johns Hopkins University, the University of Chicago, and the many state institutions across the nation assisted by the Morrill Act altered the face of higher education. There was a steady move from a religious to a secular emphasis in college curriculum; from a simple to complex form of academic organization; from a more classical curriculum to a vocational-utilitarian curriculum; from a philosophy of education for the few to education for the many; from simple literary societies to a great growth in extracurricular activities; and for the increased development of coeducational institutions, professional and graduate programs, and research activities due to the influence of the German university on American higher education.[13]

It is interesting to note that the variety of professions from which college presidents were chosen became more numerous after the Civil War. Frederick Rudolph wrote:

The clergyman president went into discard because he lacked skill in the ways of the world, because his commitment to the classical curriculum stood in the way of the more practical and popular emphasis which commended itself to the trustees, and because the world in which the colleges and universities now moved was more secular, less subject to religious influences.[14]

New Challenges

The growth of the university had taken some precedence over the older and smaller independent or sectarian college at the beginning of the twentieth century. Larger enrollments, standardization of practices, diversification of functions, and the effects of the theory of evolution and the elective system again altered the course of

12. For a discussion of this era in American higher education, see Prator, *College President,* pp. 12–13; Schmidt, *Liberal Arts,* pp. 113–23; and Rudolph, *American College,* Chapter 6.
13. Edward Blackman, Professor of Higher Education, Michigan State University, in a speech given at that institution, October 11, 1967.
14. Rudolph, *American College,* p. 419.

higher education.[15] Along with these changes, the colleges and universities required a new kind of executive officer, new methods of financing, and new areas of administration. Rudolph notes that academic presidents began to recognize themselves as belonging to a society of professionals. The office, in Veblen's phrase, called for a "captain of erudition," a manager "who could perform for higher education those functions which elsewhere in American society were being performed by the captains of industry and the captains of finance."[16]

The academic president also became more of an off-campus celebrity. Many writers mark this time as surely the end of the "old-time president." Rudolph wrote:

The capacity to lead now assumed a tremendous importance in college and university affairs. In contrast with the modern university, the old college was a place where nothing happened and where the president by a kind of indifference or remoteness or even superiority to mundane matters performed an effortless role, in seeing to it that nothing did happen. The new era, however, demanded men who knew what they wanted and, better yet, what their various publics wanted, men who were prepared to try the impossible task of being the "reconciler of irreconcilabilities," the leader to students, faculty, alumni, and trustees. . . . The collegiate or university organization was, at best, a delicate balance of interests, a polite tug of war, a blending of emphases, a disunity that found unity only through the refinements, the habits, the certainties of organization.[17]

All observers were not equally impressed with the lofty goals and image of the academic president. Upton Sinclair described the "new" university president as "the most universal faker and the most varigated prevaricator that has yet appeared in the civilized world."[18]

In the early 1900s there was increasing emphasis upon wooing alumni, benefactors, and foundations for funds. Many benefactors found their way on college boards of trustees and by using techniques that worked so well in their roles of entrepreneurs, they often alienated the professional faculty. The gap between the faculty and governing board grew steadily in many institutions and has persisted to the present.

15. Schmidt, *Liberal Arts,* p. 182.
16. Rudolph, *American College,* p. 418.
17. Ibid., p. 423.
18. Rudolph, *American College,* p. 423.

By the beginning of the First World War, the apparatus of the organized institution was complete. On one assembly line the academicians, the scholars, were at work . . . above them, around them were the managers—the white-collared, chief executive officers and their assistants. The absentee stockholders were the alumni.[19]

At the present time diversity has become the leading characteristic of institutions of American higher education, in terms of the types and sizes of institutions, their forms of control, and their stated objectives. Increasingly, and especially during the past fifteen years, the federal government has developed many-faceted relationships with colleges and universities and with their faculties, administrators, and students. All these relationships and events are far too numerous and beyond the immediate purposes to include here, but suffice it to say, the many institutions have called for various patterns of careers, training, and roles of college and university presidents. A number of authors who were former college presidents have written on various aspects of what is known of the contemporary academic president. A small sampling of their thoughts will give greater understanding into the problems and perceptions of the modern college president's career.

Henry M. Wriston reflects upon his years as president of Lawrence College and Brown University and discusses the ways in which the effective president must maintain sound relations with the trustees, the faculty, the administration, the students, and the public. Wriston, who is a strong proponent for the academic president being first of all a scholar, says: "I cannot deny that ministers, lawyers, military officers, bankers, businessmen, and others have occasionally done well. But the sound rule is that the president should be a scholar; all the other essential attributes should be present, but secondary."[20]

Harold Dodds maintains that the president's prime function is educational leadership, no matter how large or complex the institution. Dodds holds that ". . . today the need for educational statesmanship is so compelling that 50 percent of presidential time should be spent on strictly educational matters."[21]

19. Ibid., p. 423.
20. Henry M. Wriston, *Academic Procession* (New York: Columbia University Press, 1959), p. 16.
21. Harold W. Dodds, *The Academic President: Educator or Caretaker* (New York: McGraw-Hill Book Company, Inc., 1962), pp. 60–61.

Others emphasize the need for a skilled and competent administrator in handling the complex institution of today. Harold W. Stoke notes that higher education has become more secular than religious ". . . and the sheer bulk of its property, population, expenditures, and responsibilities has become an inextricable part of national living."[22] He believes that the transformation of colleges and universities reflects itself in the position of the president, ". . . and has brought to that position men whose training, interests, and skills are far different from those of their predecessors."[23] He writes:

The college president as the Man of Learning has been giving way to the Man of Management, although the change has not taken place without strain and conflict.[24]

Writers and researchers have looked at the president from a number of perspectives. Clark Kerr, former president of the University of California, offers the thesis that the president of the large, complex university system, or to use Kerr's term, the *multiversity,* must be a "mediator-innovator" rather than an "educator-leader." The president must increasingly mediate between and among the *communities* in which various groups, such as students, faculty, administrators, and the public legitimately compete for dominance and influence.[25]

In a similar vein, Demerath, Stephens, and Taylor give an account of the modern university as a "managed organization." The authors indicate that two broad streams of power exist in the academic institution: *bureaucratic* (associated with the usual line-authority relationships) and *collegial* (dealing with the interrelations of components of university government: faculty, students, and administrators). The authors note that the type of president needed for an institution depends upon the educational circumstances of the university, current administrative needs, and experiences with previous holders of the office. The heads of universities act in two theatres: one is inside their institutions (financial organization, endow-

22. Harold W. Stoke, *The American College President* (New York: Harper and Brothers, 1959), p. 2.
23. Ibid., p. 3.
24. Ibid.
25. Clark Kerr, *The Uses of the University* (Cambridge, Mass.: Harvard University Press, 1963).

ments, budget, faculty relations, student relations), and the other, outside their institutions (public relations, fund-raising, participation in state-national affairs, ceremonial head, alumni relations, legislature relations). The effective president is the one who is sensitive to both the bureaucratic and collegial aspects related to crucial decisions and policy making, and one who is able to serve the institution internally and externally as necessary.[26]

Frederick de W. Bolman has offered an analysis of the selection process of American college presidents. Bolman has found from a survey of 116 presidents of non-parochial, four-year colleges and universities—presidents who were chosen for their positions during the period 1959-1962—that the average tenure of college presidents is between ten and eleven years. This means some 200 of America's colleges and universities must seek new presidents each year. Bolman found the following regarding the careers and backgrounds of the presidents in his sample:

1) Nearly all universities insist that the president have an earned doctorate. Of the 116 recently appointed presidents, 83 per cent held earned doctorates, 61 per cent had Ph.D.s, 11 per cent had Ed.D's, and 11 per cent had other earned doctorates. Another 11 per cent had only earned the master's degree. Four per cent had the graduate Bachelor of Divinity degree, and only 2 per cent held the bachelor's degree. The doctorate is particularly important at institutions which themselves grant the Ph.D.

2) Nearly all universities want the president to be a skilled administrator and fund-raiser, but this varies among institutions.

3) Personality traits are important in the selection process as many institutions wanted presidents who could improve their institution's image, or better the relationships with members of a state legislature.

4) Most presidents are married and the wife must be a "good" wife. No matter how well qualified a candidate is in other respects, if he has an "unacceptable" wife he is seriously handicapped.[27]

In another study, John Corson found that the role of the academic president focused around six essential activities: student affairs, educational program, faculty selection, finance, physical facilities,

26. Nicholas J. Demerath, Richard W. Stephens, and R. Robb Taylor, *Power, Presidents, and Professors* (New York: Basic Books, Inc., 1967).
27. Frederick de W. Bolman, *How College Presidents Are Chosen* (American Council on Education, Washington, D.C., 1965), pp. 20–30.

and public-alumni relations. As for the president's use of time, Corson found that presidents devote approximately: 40 per cent of their time to financial-budget matters, 20 per cent of their time to public-alumni relations, 12 per cent of their time to physical facilities, 10 per cent of their time to general administration, and 18 per cent of their time to educational matters.[28] Less than one-fifth of the president's time was spent on educational matters—a finding not even close to Harold Dodd's suggested 50 per cent.

The most systematic study of a specific group of college and university presidents was conducted in 1966 by Hemphill and Walberg for the New York State Regents Advisory Committee on Educational Leadership. Their study examines the position and demands of the academic president, the background and preparation of New York college and university presidents, the effectiveness and ineffectiveness of presidents, and the recruitment and selection processes used by the state's colleges. Some of their findings that relate to the present national study include the following:

Concerning the background and preparation of presidents, the most frequent undergraduate majors of the presidents were in the humanities, followed by social sciences, engineering, physical sciences, and education. In graduate work the most frequent majors were education, humanities, and social sciences. Many presidents have participated in in-service training programs for college presidents sponsored by Harvard University, the American Management Association, or other groups, and generally find these activities helpful.

Most of the presidents held administrative positions in higher education immediately before becoming president, but more than a third held other positions, either as faculty members, as school superintendents, in state education departments, or outside the field of education.

Greater administrative experience, especially in higher education, is associated with higher effectiveness and more satisfaction in the role of president. Greater teaching experience leads to higher effectiveness but, if extensive (more than ten years), to less job satisfaction. Presidents with much teaching experience appear to retain an identification with teaching and regret that they have so little time for scholarship.

The qualifications for the presidency most often mentioned were administrative experience and college teaching experience. Other qualities, includ-

28. John J. Corson, *Governance of Colleges and Universities* (New York: McGraw-Hill Book Company, Inc., 1960), pp. 58–71.

ing physical energy, health, leadership talent, flexibility, openmindedness, sense of humor, and the ability to combat frustration, were mentioned. Presidents were divided in their opinions about the relative desirability of considering internal as well as external candidates.[29]

A summary statement of the kind of person needed for a given type of institution is presented by Ralph Prator, and the accuracy of his beliefs is tested in this book in the chapters that follow. Prator notes that ". . . the requirements of the college dictate the kind of man needed for the job . . . the qualifications for presidencies differ greatly from institution to institution and from one period in history to another."[30] For example, scholarship, research, and teaching achievement may be secondary considerations in the preparation and experience of the president of the urban-commuter college; the state college is more likely to want a scholar in the education field, and often experience in public education administration; the private church-related college president often is prominent in that particular denomination, whereas the secular college may desire a noted scholar for president. Often the college's most recent experience or problem can be an important determinant as to the qualifications desired in its president. Prator found:

In view of this diversity (in kinds of institutions in American higher education), it is unlikely that presidential qualifications will ever fall within a limited pattern. If collegiate institutions were devoted simply to excellence in teaching and the search for truth, presidents who could lead the institutions toward these two goals might have many similar qualifications. But the great range of interests, aims, states of growth and development and cultural orientations, as well as the differences in geographic location among American colleges, are reflected in the wide span of qualities required and represented in their presidents.[31]

In many respects, the background, style, and role of the academic president over the past 300 years have often reflected and adapted to the changing social, political, economic and educational climate existing in the society. In other respects, there is ample evidence that certain presidents have drawn largely upon their own capabili-

29. John K. Hemphill and Herbert Walberg, *An Empirical Study of College and University Presidents in the State of New York* (Princeton: Educational Testing Service, 1966), pp. 71–73.
30. Prator, *College President*, p. 82.
31. Prator, *College President*, pp. 84–85.

ties and have been influential in moving their institutions innovatively against an often resistant society. Although many (if not most) contemporary scholars of higher education have pointed to the general demise of the "Great Man or Hero Theory" in educational administration, it would be erroneous to view the current academic president simply as a passive, unimportant element in the operations, decisions, and activities of academia. The style of administrative-educational leadership demonstrated by an academic president, as evidenced in the literature and in the mass media, has much to do with an institution's ability to lead, adapt, and even survive, and thus the president's potential influence is still great indeed.

3

Presidential Profiles

As a clear, overall profile of the American academic president emerges from all of the research in this study it is apparent that the occupational origins of these men and women are representative of many types and levels of occupations in our society.

More American college and university presidents come from professional and executive backgrounds than from lower level occupations, the only exceptions being presidents of Catholic institutions whose fathers held lower and medium level positions. When the occupations of the presidents' fathers are compared to the general male population, the five occupational groups overrepresented are: professional, minor business executive, major business executive, government civil service, and military service. Four occupational groups which are underrepresented are: farmer, skilled laborer, white collar worker, and unskilled or semi-skilled laborer.

Geographical Origins

The geographical origins of academic presidents show representation from all regions of the country, although there is evidence that the presidents were physically as well as occupationally mobile during their careers. About 40 per cent of the academic presidents in this research were born in rural communities under 2,500 and another 20 per cent were from small towns under 25,000. While presidents of non-Catholic institutions come more frequently from rural communities or small towns, the presidents of Catholic institutions come more often from large urban areas. Only about 4 per cent of the presidents were foreign-born. More similarities than differences are found among the occupational and geographical origins of academic presidents, although presidents of similar types of institutions show the greatest similarities. The origins of presidents of either public institutions, Catholic institutions, Protestant-related institutions, independent institutions, or technological institutions appear quite similar while there are noticeable differences between the presidents of different types of institutions. Throughout the president's life and career, there was a tendency to be associated with a particular type of institution (public or private)—where he received his higher education, where he taught, and where he ultimately became president—rather than a mixing of different types of institutions.

Family Influences

An examination of the paternal grandfathers' occupations reveals that 43 per cent were farmers; relatively large percentages were laborers, white collar workers, and professionals. Occupational succession from the presidents' grandfathers to the fathers was characterized by a general movement from the farm to the city and from lower-level business positions to higher-level business positions. The presidents' fathers moved not only to somewhat larger urban communities, but to colleges where nearly one-third prepared for professional careers. The great majority of the presidents' parents and grandparents were born in the United States, except for the parents of Catholic institution presidents where larger percentages were foreign-born. Nearly 45 per cent of the presidents' parents did not graduate from high school, but 27 per cent of the fathers were college graduates and 17 per cent received graduate degrees. The wives of college and university presidents (and only 2 per cent of the presidents of non-Catholic institutions are not married) come from similar occupational levels as the presidents themselves, although relatively more of the wives' fathers were in higher level business positions and fewer were in professional fields.

Higher Education

The academic presidents were educated in a great variety of institutions at different degree levels, and nearly three-fourths earned an academic doctorate, with the doctor of philosophy (Ph.D.) the most prevalent degree among all presidents. Other important degrees earned were: the doctor of education or Ed.D. (especially for presidents of public liberal arts colleges); the doctor of sacred theology or S.T.D. (for presidents of Catholic institutions); and the bachelor of divinity or B.D. (for presidents of Protestant-related institutions). Few presidents terminated their education at the bachelor degree level, and among presidents selected to their positions in 1967–68, over 80 per cent had earned a doctorate. The presidents majored in nearly all types of curricula, but about half took undergraduate degrees in the humanities. At the master's degree level, humanities still led, followed by education, social science, and natural science. At the doctoral level, 37 per cent majored in humanities, 30 per cent in education, 14 per cent in social science, 13 per cent in natural science, and the remaining in applied fields. Although presidents studied at a great variety of institutions, only sixteen universities were attended by nearly 58 per cent of the presidents at the doctoral level. The four universities of Chicago, Columbia, Harvard, and Catholic University, granted academic doctorates to nearly one-fourth of all presidents in the sample. The few presidents who studied abroad attended the universities of Oxford, Cambridge, Rome, and Toronto. About 23 per cent of all the presidents in this study are alumni of the institutions they now head, while nearly one-half of all Catholic institution presidents are alumni of the institutions they now head.

Career Patterns

The majority of presidents spent their full-time careers in education and professional fields. Over a twenty-year period in their careers, there were steady movements into higher levels of academic administration and by the twenty-year point, about 63 per cent had attained the presidency. Academic presidents attained their present positions at about the age of forty-five and their current age is fifty-three (on the average). The "average" academic president has been in his present position for about eight years. About 86 per cent of the presidents have had prior experiences as college teachers, and approximately 60 per cent attained the rank of full professor. About one-fourth of the presidents had been college teachers for ten years or less, while 21 percent had over fifteen years college teaching experience. About 82 per cent who were college teachers were associated with twelve academic departments led by English, educational administration, history, and religion. The presidents taught at a variety of institutions at each academic rank, but 36 per cent taught at the institution they now head.

About one-third of the presidents moved to the presidency from within their present institution while two-thirds moved directly to the presidency from outside the institution. Over three-fourths moved directly from within the general field of education, led by positions as college dean (22 per cent), academic vice-president (11 per cent), department chairman (11 per cent), and college faculty (10 per cent). Business directly supplied only 2 per cent of academic presidents; 3 per cent came from government, 1 per cent from the military, and 1 per cent from foundations. It is likely that the president held his prior position about five and one-half years. Academic presidents generally have had full-time faculty or administrative positions in two other institutions, and although nearly one-third of these people were selected to their positions without full-time academic administrative experience, most of them had about ten years of such experience. About 12 per cent of the presidents had been presidents of other colleges or universities.

Career Perceptions

Academic presidents believe they were motivated to follow a career in higher educational administration and the presidency due mainly to six interrelated orientations: a service orientation, social influences, professional opportunities, personal factors, a developmental process, and accidental circumstance. In most cases, presidents chose careers in higher education, primarily as teachers, and then a series of activities and decisions of increased responsibilities and involvement in the administration of first, a department and then a college, led to the presidency. Based upon particular values, philosophies, needs, and circumstances, they were chosen or selected to head an institution. Few prefer to say they actually chose or systematically planned for a career in academic administration. Most presidents seem to be quite satisfied with their positions while some are eagerly anticipating a return to the classroom.

A Comparative Analysis

The occupational origins of academic presidents are quite similar to those of business and government leaders, with disproportionately higher representation in the professions and high level business positions. All elites, however, include persons of relatively lower occupational origins. The academic presidents are more representative of the national population, in terms of their geographical origins and sizes of hometowns, than their counterparts in business and government. While the business and government leaders have come primarily from large urban areas, the academic presidents are more likely to have come from small towns or rural communities. While the fathers of business and government leaders moved from farms to cities, it is apparent that fathers of academic presidents moved from farms to small towns and to colleges to prepare for professions. Among all leaders, a very large percentage of their grandfathers were farmers. Academic presidents are more formally educated than business and government leaders, with six American universities listed among each elite's top ten in the number of degrees received. The average business leader assumed his present position at the age of 45.3 years and was, at the time of the Warner study, 53.7 years old; the average federal executive assumed his present position at the age of 44.8 and at the time of the research he was 49.4; the average academic president assumed his present position at the age of 45.1 and at the time of this study is 52.9. Relatively few women were found among the government leaders; the eighty-four female college presidents head either Catholic liberal arts colleges or other private colleges for women.

In the preceding paragraphs the focus was upon the careers of academic presidents in general, thus it was inevitable that some of the more interesting and diverse career patterns that are associated with presidents of different types of institutions were omitted. The following summaries are aimed at highlighting these differences; brief descriptive career profiles for the presidents of nine basic four-year institutions have been developed from the text, and the central tendencies have been used to indicate only the most general patterns for each.

Profile of:
Public University Presidents

The fathers of public university presidents were mostly professional men, farmers, small businessmen, or laborers—in that order. The presidents were born in all regions of the country, although one-fourth were born in the East North Central states. One-half the presidents were born in rural communities while one-fourth were born in cities over 100,000. Their paternal grandfathers were mainly farmers or professional men, while their mothers' fathers were either farmers or small businessmen. Thirty per cent of their fathers and 14 per cent of their mothers were college graduates. Their fathers-in-law were major business executives, large business owners, or professional men.

The most typical degree earned was the Ph.D., and a majority studied humanities or education at a state university. About one-third were Phi Beta Kappas. The public university presidents are about fifty-four years of age, and they have been in their present positions about seven years. They usually began their careers as college teachers or high school teachers and most of them reached the presidency within twenty years after their first full-time positions. They earned the rank of professor and taught for about fifteen years in state universities. They moved directly to the presidency from a college deanship, academic vice-presidency (provost), or presidency of another public university. They had slightly more than ten years full-time administrative experience prior to accepting the presidency.

Profile of:
Catholic University Presidents

The fathers of Catholic university presidents were most likely major business executives or were in minor business executive positions. More than one-half the presidents were born in New York, Pennsylvania, or Illinois; most were born in large cities and none came from rural communities. It was most typical for their paternal and maternal grandfathers to be small business owners, skilled laborers, or foremen. Their parents were high school graduates.

More than one-half the presidents earned Ph.D.s and another 20 per cent earned S.T.D.s at Catholic universities, most often at Catholic University, Fordham, and Rome. About one-third earned undergraduate degrees at the institutions they now head. Average age of the presidents is about fifty-one years; they have been in their present positions about seven years. They chose religious careers and began their work as college teachers and administrators. In less than fifteen years, a majority were requested by their religious superiors to assume the presidency. An equal percentage earned faculty ranks of professor or assistant professor and a majority spent less than ten years as college teachers. They moved directly to the presidency from a college deanship, academic or administrative vice-presidency, or departmental chairmanship, at a Catholic university, a position they held for about five years. In the vast majority of cases, the move to the presidency was an internal one within the institution. Before accepting the presidency the Catholic university presidents had about seven years experience as full-time educational administrators.

Profile of:
Protestant-Related University Presidents

The majority of fathers of Protestant-related university presidents were farmers or clergymen. About one-half the presidents were born in the North Central states in rural communities or small towns. Their paternal grandfathers were either farmers or small businessmen, and their maternal grandfathers were either farmers, ministers, or lower level business employees. Their parents tended to be high school graduates, with some having college religious degrees. Their fathers-in-law tended to be farmers and professional men.

The majority of the presidents earned doctor of philosophy degrees, while a few held the bachelor of divinity or master of arts degrees. They studied the humanities at mainly private universities and over one-fourth were Phi Beta Kappas. Their average age is about fifty-eight and they have been in their present positions about thirteen years. (They are a little older on the average than other academic presidents and have had longer tenures than the others.) While most began their careers as college teachers, over one-fourth began as ministers. About three-fourths have had college teaching experience, with most attaining the rank of professor while teaching some twelve years at private institutions. They moved directly to the presidency from an academic or administrative vice-presidency, other college presidency, or college deanship in a private institution. A few came directly from pastorates. Most presidents were in their most recent positions about seven years and few moved to the presidency from within the same institution. About one-third of the presidents had never had full-time educational administrative experience prior to assuming the presidency.

Profile of:
Independent University Presidents

The fathers of independent university presidents came mainly from positions as major business executives, business owners, lawyers and the clergy. Nearly one-half of the presidents in this category were born in the New England and Middle Atlantic states, and about one-third came from large cities. Their paternal and maternal grandfathers were most likely farmers, professional men, small business owners, and skilled laborers. Forty-five per cent of the fathers and 29 per cent of their mothers were college graduates. Their fathers-in-law were predominantly small business owners, professional men, and major business executives.

Nearly three-fourths of these presidents earned Ph.D. degrees majoring in the humanities and physical sciences; nearly all received their degrees at private universities in the New England and Middle Atlantic states. About one-third were Phi Beta Kappas. Their average age is about fifty-three years and they have been in their present positions for about five and one-half years. About 40 per cent began their careers as college teachers and about 20 per cent were secondary teachers. Over 90 per cent had college teaching experience, the great majority of whom were full professors. Most were college teachers for about eleven years in private universities and liberal arts colleges. They moved directly to the presidency from an academic vice-presidency (provost), another college presidency, department chairmanship, and college deanship in private universities. In seven out of ten cases, the move was external or from outside the institution. They had on the average ten years of full-time educational administrative experience before assuming the position.

Profile of:
Public Liberal Arts College Presidents

The fathers of public liberal arts presidents came from a great variety of occupational levels, but the majority were farmers, small business owners, and lower level business employees. These presidents were born in all regions of the nation, and 72 per cent were born in communities with under 10,000 people (only one in ten came from a large city). Nearly one-half of their paternal and maternal grandfathers were farmers with large percentages as laborers and small business owners. Relatively few of their parents were college graduates and their fathers-in-law were engaged in all levels of business.

About 90 per cent had earned an academic doctorate led by 50 per cent with a doctor of philosophy degree and 37 per cent with a doctor of education degree. They majored in education and humanities at state universities throughout the country. Only 12 per cent earned degrees at institutions over which they preside and 11 per cent were Phi Beta Kappas, although nearly two-thirds were members of other honoraries—usually educational. Their average age is fifty-three and they have been in their present positions for about eight years. Approximately 60 per cent began their careers as public school teachers and 14 per cent began as college teachers. Within fifteen years, about one-fourth were college presidents. Most had college teaching experience—often teaching educational administration— and about 60 per cent attained the rank of professor. Their average

college teaching experience was thirteen years while teaching in
state colleges and universities. The most prominent springboard to
the presidency was overwhelmingly a college deanship, but other
important positions were department chairman, member of a
college faculty, and public school superintendent, nearly all in
public education. Prior to assuming the presidency, the average
public liberal arts president had ten years of full-time educational
administrative experience.

Profile of:
Catholic Liberal Arts College Presidents

Like the fathers of Catholic university presidents, the fathers of
liberal arts presidents were usually in all levels of the business hierarchy, mainly at middle and lower levels. Most of the presidents
were born in large urban areas of New York, Pennsylvania, Illinois,
Massachusetts, and Minnesota. Their paternal and maternal grandfathers were also in business occupations with nearly 40 per cent in
unskilled and skilled laborer levels. Their parents were usually high
school graduates.

About seven out of ten presidents earned a doctorate, usually the
Ph.D., while almost one-fourth terminated their formal education at
the master's level. They usually studied humanities (religion) and
earned degrees at Catholic universities such as Catholic University,
St. Louis, Fordham, and Notre Dame. Nearly 45 per cent had
earned undergraduate degrees at the colleges they now head. The
presidents have an average age of fifty-one and most were about
forty-four years of age when their religious superiors asked them to
assume the presidency. About 46 per cent began their careers, following acceptance into a religious order, in teaching at elementary-
secondary levels of Catholic education, while 18 per cent began as
college teachers. Over 92 per cent had college teaching experience,
and a majority taught less than ten years and attained the ranks of
assistant or associate professor. Nearly 80 per cent taught at the
institution they now head. Three positions were the basic springboards to the presidency: college deanship, department chairman, or
faculty member in a Catholic college. While nearly 50 per cent had
no full-time educational administrative experience prior to the presidency, those who did were in such positions for about nine years.

Profile of:

Protestant-Related Liberal Arts College Presidents

The fathers of Protestant-related liberal arts presidents were primarily clergymen, farmers, skilled laborers and small business owners. These presidents were usually born in Pennsylvania and the North Central states, often in small communities. Their paternal and maternal grandfathers were mainly farmers, small business owners, and skilled laborers. About 30 per cent of their fathers and 16 per cent of their mothers were college graduates. Their fathers-in-law were predominantly farmers, professional men (ministers), small business owners, and major business executives.

About 60 per cent earned doctorates (usually the Ph.D.), while almost one in ten earned a bachelor of divinity degree. The presidents majored in humanities usually at public and private universities in the East North Central, Middle Atlantic, and South Atlantic states. About 22 per cent earned undergraduate degrees at their present institutions. The presidents have an average age of fifty-two and they have been in their present positions about eight years. These presidents began their careers in three basic levels: as ministers, elementary-secondary teachers, and college faculty members. About 72 per cent have had college teaching experience while 42 per cent attained the rank of professor. A majority taught about twelve years in private, coeducational liberal arts colleges. The presidents moved directly to their present positions from three principal positions: as ministers, college deans, and college faculty members (in that order). They were mainly involved in Protestant-related liberal arts colleges, and they held full-time administrative positions about ten years before assuming the presidency. For those who came from ministerial positions, the presidency offered an opportunity for an enlarged and extended ministry.

Profile of:

Independent Liberal Arts College Presidents

The fathers of independent liberal arts college presidents were mainly professional men, major business executives, and small business owners. Most of these presidents were born in New York, Pennsylvania, Illinois, and Minnesota—in large urban communities.

Their paternal and maternal grandfathers most often were farmers, small business owners, skilled laborers, and clergymen. Almost one-half of the fathers and 37 per cent of the mothers were college graduates. Their fathers-in-law were most likely small business owners and major business executives.

The independent liberal arts presidents usually earned Ph.D.s in humanities in private universities in New England, East North Central, and Middle Atlantic states. About 37 per cent (the highest of any group of presidents) were Phi Beta Kappas. The presidents are on the average fifty-three years of age, and they have been in their present positions about nine and one-half years. It was most likely that they began their careers as college faculty members while some were elementary teachers. More than 93 per cent had college teaching experience with one-half of these people attaining the rank of full professor in departments of English and history. About one-half of the presidents in this category were teachers for more than ten years at private institutions. The springboard to the presidency was from a college deanship or faculty position in a non-sectarian institution. The president had an average of ten years full-time educational administrative experience prior to assuming the presidency.

Profile of:
Technological Institution Presidents

The fathers of technological institution presidents tended to be engaged in business activities and farming. The presidents were born in Middle Atlantic and North Central states in rural communities or in big cities. Their paternal and maternal grandfathers were mainly farmers, foremen, and skilled laborers. About 32 per cent of the fathers and about 20 per cent of the mothers were college graduates. Their fathers-in-law were primarily small business owners, skilled laborers, and engineers.

About eight in ten received a doctorate in the physical sciences or education, about equally at public and private universities in the Middle Atlantic and East North Central regions. The presidents' average age is nearly fifty-five and they have been in their positions about eight years. These presidents were likely to have begun their careers as college or secondary teachers and nearly all had college teaching experiences, the majority attaining the rank of full professor. They taught engineering courses, chemistry, or physics for about thirteen years at private and public universities and technological institutions. Their direct move to the presidency came from a department chairmanship, college deanship, academic vice-presidency or college faculty position at a public liberal arts college or independent university. Prior to assuming their present positions, they had about ten years administrative experience in education.

4

Origins

The question of occupational succession provides the initial focus in reviewing research findings of this study. Whether college and university presidents in general tend to come from similar or different occupational origins is a chief concern. Do the occupational origins of public university presidents differ from the origins of private university presidents or from the origins of public and private liberal arts college presidents? It can be learned whether the fathers of academic presidents seem to be representative of the various occupational groups in the general population or whether the fathers come largely from the more elite occupations and occupational levels.

Occupational Origins

Classification of seven general occupations subdivided into twenty specific occupations of the fathers at the time when the presidents began their full time occupational careers is presented in Table 1.[1]

This table shows that the fathers of university presidents were engaged in all types and levels of occupations. Fathers who were in the professions are generally more prevalent, with the exception of the fathers of Catholic university presidents. From 33 to 45 per cent of the fathers of public and private, non-Catholic university presidents were engaged in professional work at the time their sons began full-time careers.

More than 50 per cent of the fathers of public university presidents in this study were either professional men or farmers; about 30 per cent were either business executives or business owners, with a larger concentration in minor executive and small business ownership positions. About 10 per cent of the fathers were in the general laborer category, a majority being skilled workers. It is interesting to note that not one father was a white-collar worker and only a few were in military service or in civil service positions.

The fathers of Catholic university presidents stand out markedly from the others when occupational positions are considered; only 10 per cent were in the traditional professions, and none of these men were in the field of education. Over 50 per cent were either business executives or business owners, and a majority were major executives or owners of large businesses. In comparison to the fathers of public university presidents, a larger percentage of the fathers of Catholic university presidents were in the laborer and white-collar categories (almost 30 per cent). None of the fathers of Catholic university presidents were farmers. The occupational origins of Catholic university presidents represent all levels of the business sector in greater proportions than is true among all other presidents. In fact, 85 per cent of the fathers of Catholic university presidents were employed in the general business area.

The presidents of Protestant-related universities appear similar to

1. Since the methodology for this study was purposely kept similar to the Warner studies, these general categories were taken from that research, and information on the fathers of academic presidents was reorganized to permit cross-comparisons. To show contrasts among the presidents, the occupations of the fathers are correlated with the type of institution the president heads, and then a composite profile of all types of presidents is shown in tabular form. This particular style of presenting data by institutional type is followed throughout much of the report and will be complemented by other categories (for example, sex of respondent, size of institution, regional location of the institution) whenever additional insights are made possible by such an exposition.

TABLE 1

<small>UNIVERSITY PRESIDENTS: DISTRIBUTION OF FATHERS' OCCUPATIONS</small>

Father's Occupation	*Percentage of Distribution by Father's Occupation*				
	Public (n = 87)	Catholic (n = 20)	Prot.-Related (n = 20)	Independent (n = 29)	Total (n = 156)
Laborer	**10.3**	**20.0**	**10.0**	**3.4**	**10.2**
Unskilled, semiskilled	2.3	10.0	5.0	3.4	3.8
Skilled, mechanic	8.0	10.0	5.0	0.0	6.4
White-Collar					
Clerk, salesman	**0.0**	**10.0**	**5.0**	**6.9**	**3.2**
Business Executive	**13.8**	**35.0**	**10.0**	**24.1**	**18.0**
Foreman, minor executive	6.9	15.0	5.0	13.8	9.0
Major executive	6.9	20.0	5.0	10.3	9.0
Business Owner	**16.0**	**20.0**	**5.0**	**13.8**	**14.5**
Small-firm	12.6	5.0	5.0	0.0	8.2
Large business	3.4	15.0	0.0	13.8	6.3
Professional	**32.0**	**10.0**	**40.0**	**44.7**	**33.1**
Physician	2.3	0.0	0.0	3.4	1.9
Engineer	2.3	0.0	5.0	3.4	2.6
Lawyer	5.7	5.0	0.0	13.8	6.4
Clergyman	6.9	0.0	30.0	13.8	10.1
Elementary-secondary teacher	6.9	0.0	0.0	6.9	5.1
College faculty	2.2	0.0	0.0	0.0	1.3
College dean or vice-president	0.0	0.0	5.0	0.0	1.3
College president	0.0	0.0	0.0	3.4	0.6
Other	5.7	5.0	0.0	0.0	3.8
Farmer, including workers or owners	**19.5**	**0.0**	**30.0**	**6.9**	**16.0**
Other Occupations	**7.9**	**5.0**	**0.0**	**0.0**	**5.0**
Military	1.1	0.0	0.0	0.0	0.6
Government, primarily civil service	5.7	5.0	0.0	0.0	3.8
Other	1.1	0.0	0.0	0.0	0.6
Total per cent	100.0*	100.0	100.0	100.0	100.0

*Does not total 100 per cent exactly due to rounding of figures.

public university presidents in comparing their fathers' occupations; 70 per cent of their fathers were professional men and farmers. (A more striking aspect of this finding is that about 30 per cent of the fathers were clergymen.) None of the fathers were in the military or government civil service and only a small percentage were business owners, business executives, white-collar workers or laborers. A total of 30 per cent were spread over the various levels of the business hierarchy.

Fathers of the presidents of private independent universities were primarily in professional fields (nearly 45 per cent) and the business executive category (24 per cent). Only 3 per cent were unskilled or skilled laborers while nearly 25 per cent were either major executives or large business owners. None of the fathers had careers in military or government civil service and only 7 per cent were farmers.

In developing a profile of all university presidents, public and private, we see that about one-third have professional origins, led by fathers who were clergymen, lawyers, and elementary-secondary teachers. The second highest general category for all university presidents is that of business executive, followed by farming and business ownership. About 10 per cent of all fathers were laborers, the majority in skilled work, and only 3 per cent were in white-collar employment. As a general category, only 5 per cent of the fathers were in military or government civil service.

Thus, there is a predominance of professional origins for all university presidents, with the exception of Catholic university presidents whose fathers were largely engaged in business activities. For all, there is a relatively small number and percentage who were engaged in education, especially at the college level.

Out of all the university presidents in the study, only one reported that his father was a college president, and only about 3 per cent had fathers who were college faculty members.

While it is interesting to examine these statistics, it is possible to gain an even greater insight into whether the occupational origins of university presidents are truly representative of American society, and if not, the nature and extent of the deviations. The question becomes: Are forces at work within the society that give certain occupational groups a greater share of higher educational top leadership than their proportion in the general population? To answer this question, the following methodology, used similarly by the Warner researches, was employed.

The average age of the academic presidents was found to be approximately fifty-three in 1968. Since most of the presidents attended college for a varying number of years and academic degrees, the average age of beginning full-time work was estimated to be about twenty-three. Therefore, the occupations of the fathers are given, again on the average, for about 1938, or close to the 1940 census of population. Any comparisons then would be between the occupations of the adult male population in 1940 and the fathers of the academic presidents. Table 2 summarizes the comparisons.

University Presidents

Comparisons shown in Table 2 provide evidence of the under-representation or overrepresentation of ten basic occupational classifications among university presidents. (The structuring of the table was developed to account for the way the 1940 United States census data were categorized and caused some necessary reorganization of the occupations given in the questionnaire.) By contrasting the column that summarizes all university presidents with

TABLE 2
UNIVERSITY PRESIDENTS: PROPORTIONAL REPRESENTATION RATIOS
OF FATHERS' OCCUPATIONS

Father's Occupation	All Presidents (per cent)	Total Population[b] (per cent)	Ratio of Fathers to All Males	Rank Order of Overrepresentation
Unskilled laborer	4	31	0.13	10
Skilled laborer	6	14	0.43	8
Clerk, sales (white-collar)	3	13	0.23	9
Foreman	9	2	4.50	2
Executive, manager, proprietor[a]	24	10	2.40	4
Professional	33	5	6.60	1
Farmer	16	22	0.73	7
Government	4	1	4.00	3
Military	1	1	1.00	5
Other	1	1	1.00	6
Total per cent	100	100		

[a] Includes major business executives and small and large business owners.
[b] U.S. Male Adult Population, 1910, Bureau of the Census, Vol. 1, pp. 75–80.

the United States male population, it can be seen that while about 31 per cent of the 1940 male population were unskilled or semi-skilled laborers, only 4 per cent of the university presidents are the sons of unskilled or semiskilled laborers. However, while only 5 per cent of the U.S. male population were considered in the professional category, some 33 per cent of the university presidents are sons of professionals. As Warner noted in his studies and is also readily apparent here, the difference in these comparative proportions is a measure of the underrepresentation of the sons of laborers and the overrepresentation of the sons of professionals. A simple ratio of the proportion of each occupational group among the university presidents to that in the U.S. male population of 1940 gives an exact measurement of which groups are over and underrepresented. Thus, a ratio of 1.00 signifies an occupation which is equally represented among university president's fathers and in the total male population.

The percentage of university presidents whose fathers were in professional fields was nearly seven times the proportion of that group in the general U.S. male population. The most underrepresented group is the unskilled or semiskilled laborer with a ratio of only 0.13, meaning that there seems to have been very limited mobility of the sons of the unskilled to the university presidency. The next most underrepresented occupational groups are the white-collar (clerk, sales) workers (0.23), skilled laborers (0.43), and farmers (0.73), while there is a perfect representation among those in military service (1.00). The overrepresented groups include business executives, managers, and proprietors (2.40), those in government civil service (4.00), foremen (4.50), and professional fields (6.60). Thus, the 1968 university presidents (with some variations associated with presidents of particular types of institutions) are in large part the sons of men of fairly high occupational status, such as the sons of professional men and business managers, but they are also the sons of men of lower occupational status, such as foremen and minor executives in business and government.

While there is evidence for most mobility to be across the long-held professions into higher education, there is still an element of movement upward from the lower occupational classes to higher educational administration. Although five occupational groups are overrepresented and four are underrepresented, all are found among university presidents.[2]

2. The reader is advised that it will be necessary at times to separate the data of presidents of Catholic institutions from the others only in order to accurately represent the careers of these presidents and all others. It should be recognized (and will be given more elaboration in later chapters) that all heads of Catholic institutions in the sample were not only educators but also members of the priesthood and various religious orders. For purposes of this study, their educational leadership position in the society has been the central concern, and any discussion of social origins, education, and career patterns has hopefully been focused upon and related essentially to their educational position and career, not to their intricately bound missions and careers as priests or sisters. Obviously, this has not been an easy task to accomplish.

Catholic University Presidents

Catholic university presidents generally show more distance covered in upward occupational mobility than the total group. Specially formulated ratios for the fathers of Catholic university presidents indicate the same four groups underrepresented, but not by as much—for example, unskilled or semiskilled laborers, 0.32; skilled laborers, 0.71; white-collar workers, 0.77; while there was no mobility from the farmers category, 0.00. For those overrepresented, the foremen class is highest with a ratio of 7.50; government civil service, 5.00; business managers, 4.00; and professionals are reduced to a ratio of 2.00.

Liberal Arts College Presidents

The same presentation of the general and specific occupational groups is given in Table 3, but here attention is focused upon the occupations of the fathers of the individuals who head the nation's liberal arts colleges. It should be kept in mind that of the nearly 600 liberal arts college presidents in the study, about 14 per cent (or eighty-four) are women, the great majority of whom are found in seventy-three women's Catholic liberal arts colleges. This has some bearing in trying to understand the career patterns of Catholic liberal arts college presidents as well as in assessing the meaning of their occupational origins.

Liberal arts college presidents represent all occupational origins, although just as it was true with university presidents, there are variations associated with presidents of different types of colleges. Initially it should be seen that the professional category is well represented among most liberal arts college presidents as it is among university presidents. Professional and farmer categories account for more than 45 per cent of the occupational origins of the presidents of public liberal arts colleges. A fairly large percentage of fathers are also found in the laborer class (17 per cent) with more than two-thirds being skilled workers. Fathers who were business managers and owners comprise about one-fourth of the public college presidents, with major executive statuses and ownership in small rather than large businesses being the rule. The small entrepreneur category is well represented among the origins of public college presi-

TABLE 3
LIBERAL ARTS PRESIDENTS: DISTRIBUTION OF FATHERS' OCCUPATIONS

	Percentage of Distribution by Father's Occupation					
Father's Occupation	Public (n = 144)	Catholic (n = 125)	Protes- tant (n = 205)	Indepen- dent (n = 73)	Techno- logical (n = 29)	Total (n = 576)
Laborer	**17.4**	**28.0**	**16.1**	**9.6**	**6.8**	**17.6**
Unskilled, semiskilled	4.2	13.6	5.9	5.5	3.4	6.9
Skilled, mechanic	13.2	14.4	10.2	4.1	3.4	10.7
White-Collar						
Clerk, salesman	**4.2**	**8.8**	**3.9**	**1.4**	**6.8**	**4.9**
Business Executive	**9.8**	**18.4**	**11.8**	**12.3**	**6.8**	**12.6**
Foreman, minor executive	3.5	12.0	5.9	2.7	6.8	6.3
Major executive	6.3	6.4	5.9	9.6	0.0	6.3
Business Owner	**16.7**	**15.2**	**9.3**	**12.3**	**17.0**	**13.2**
Small firm	13.9	12.8	8.8	8.2	13.6	11.1
Large business	2.8	2.4	0.5	4.1	3.4	2.1
Professional	**24.5**	**12.8**	**39.3**	**47.8**	**23.8**	**30.0**
Physician	0.7	0.8	1.5	6.8	0.0	1.7
Engineer	4.2	3.2	2.0	1.4	6.8	3.0
Lawyer	1.4	4.0	0.5	4.1	0.0	1.9
Clergyman	4.9	0.0	22.0	16.4	3.4	11.1
Elementary-secondary teacher	5.6	0.0	4.9	0.0	6.8	3.5
College faculty	0.7	0.0	1.5	5.5	0.0	1.4
College dean or vice-president	2.8	0.0	1.5	2.7	0.0	1.6
College president	1.4	0.0	2.0	2.7	3.4	1.6
Other	2.8	4.8	3.4	8.2	3.4	4.2
Farmer	**21.5**	**9.6**	**16.6**	**11.0**	**24.0**	**16.0**
Other Occupations	**6.3**	**7.2**	**3.5**	**5.5**	**13.6**	**5.7**
Military	0.7	1.6	0.0	1.4	10.2	1.2
Government	5.6	4.8	3.0	4.1	3.4	4.2
Other	0.0	0.8	0.5	0.0	0.0	0.3
Total per cent	100.0*	100.0	100.0*	100.0*	100.0*	100.0

*Does not total 100 per cent exactly due to rounding of figures.

dents. Of those fathers who were professionals, more than 10 per cent were in education, split about evenly at the secondary and college levels.

Catholic college presidents (56 per cent of whom are women) come more frequently from laborer occupational origins, equally from the unskilled and skilled occupations. Fathers who were business executives and owners are also represented among the Catholic college presidents. It is important to note, however, that a majority of those who were executives were foremen or other minor executives while over 85 per cent of the owners were found in small or medium-sized business firms. As was true with Catholic university presidents, a relatively small percentage of fathers of the college presidents were in professional fields, about 13 per cent, and none were in education. Also, a small percentage of fathers were farmers or involved in military and government civil service. No significant differences were found in comparing the fathers' occupations between the men and women who head the Catholic liberal arts colleges. The priests and nuns had similar occupational origins.

Among the many presidents of private, Protestant-related liberal arts colleges, there are a large number of fathers from professional fields (40 per cent). And, as it was with the Protestant-related university presidents, many fathers were clergymen (22 per cent). Another 10 per cent of the fathers were in education, equally divided in elementary-secondary ranks and in colleges. About 16 per cent of the fathers were laborers, a majority being skilled, and another 4 per cent of the fathers were clerical and sales employees. Business executives and owners accounted for 20 per cent of the occupational origins of the presidents, with virtually all business owners found in small or medium-sized businesses. Almost 17 per cent of the fathers were farmers and only 3 per cent were in government civil service.

The strongest proportional representation of the professional category is found among the fathers of the private, independent liberal arts college presidents (corresponding to the high professional percentage for presidents of private independent universities). Nearly one-half of these presidents had fathers who were engaged in professional endeavors. The leading professions of the fathers of independent liberal arts college presidents were: clergymen, 16 per cent; college faculty, 8 per cent; and almost 3 per cent of the presidents had fathers who were college presidents. A relatively small number of presidents have their origins in farming occupations (11 per cent) and 5 per cent had fathers in military and government service. Almost one-fourth of the fathers were business executives and owners, with the concentration in major executive positions and ownership of smaller businesses. About 10 per cent of the fathers were laborers and another 1 per cent of the fathers were white-collar workers.

The fathers of the presidents of the technological institutions were found in all occupational groups and about one-fourth were professionals. (In the professional category, almost 7 per cent were engineers and another 7 per cent were secondary teachers.) Another one-fourth of the fathers were farmers followed by 17 per cent who were business owners in primarily smaller business establishments. Stronger representation in military service origins is found among these presidents, owing largely to the fact that of the four military college presidents, two had fathers in military service. An equal percentage of fathers were found in positions as laborer, white collar worker, and minor executive.

In view of the totals for all five types of college presidents, there is no question that professional occupational origins dominate with 30 per cent of the fathers having such careers. Further down the list, in order, are laborers, 18 per cent; farmers, 16 per cent; business owners, 13 per cent; and business executives, 13 per cent. Catholic college presidents as a group, however, tend to appear quite different in occupational origins from their colleagues in the other colleges. Such differences are quite consistent with the origins of Catholic university presidents, except more lower level business origins in smaller firms are found among the college presidents, and a larger percentage of college presidents come from farming backgrounds. Among all groups of college presidents only 8 per cent of their fathers were professional educators, and only nine presidents had fathers who were college presidents.

It is seen in the tables that the most disadvantaged groups in terms of representation among the liberal arts college presidents are unskilled or semiskilled laborers (with a ratio of 0.23) followed by three other underrepresented groups: white-collar workers, 0.38; farmers, 0.73; and skilled laborers, 0.79. Overrepresented groups are led by the professional fields with six times the representation than would be expected from the general population, followed by government civil service, 4.00; foremen, 3.00; and executives, managers, and proprietors, 2.00.

Catholic Liberal Arts Presidents

If the fathers of Catholic liberal arts college presidents are considered separately since they tend to differ significantly from the others, only three occupational groups are disadvantaged (but not as greatly as in the total college president group): unskilled or semiskilled laborers, 0.41; farmers, 0.45; and white collar workers, 0.69. The most overrepresented occupational origins among Catholic college presidents are foremen with 6.00, followed by those in government civil service, 5.00; professional men, 2.60; executives, managers, and proprietors, 2.10; military service, 2.00; and skilled laborers, 1.00. In the Catholic colleges, there is again evidence of more distance covered in upward occupational mobility to higher educational leadership. In addition, although the non-Catholic college president moved across, in general, from professional origins, he also moved up from minor executive positions in business and government in greater proportion than would be expected on the basis of the general population.

TABLE 4

LIBERAL ARTS PRESIDENTS: PROPORTIONAL REPRESENTATION RATIOS
OF FATHERS' OCCUPATIONS

Father's Occupation	All Presidents (per cent)	Total Population (per cent)	Ratio of Fathers to All Males	Rank Order of Over-representation
Unskilled laborer	7	31	0.23	9
Skilled laborer	11	14	0.79	6
Clerk, sales	5	13	0.38	8
Foreman	6	2	3.00	3
Executive, manager, proprietor	20	10	2.00	4
Professional	30	5	6.00	1
Farmer	16	22	0.73	7
Government	4	1	4.00	2
Military	1	1	1.00	5
Other	0	1	0.00	10

The professions have been important sources of leadership among college and university presidents. Comparisons were made between the percentage of males in seven major professional groups in the 1940 census and the percentages found among the 1968 college and university president elite, as shown in Table 5. In terms of the relative size of the general population, the single profession of the clergy ranks higher (with a ratio of 28.46) than any other group, although the classification of elementary and secondary teachers is not far behind, with a ratio of 23.75. If this procedure could be used among more specific occupations in the other general categories, perhaps other occupations might have an equal or higher ratio, but census

TABLE 5
PROFESSIONS OF THE FATHERS OF ACADEMIC PRESIDENTS

Father's Profession	Percentage of U.S. Population*	Percentage of Presidents' Fathers	Proportional Representation Ratio
Physician	0.46	1.8	3.91
Engineer	0.80	2.9	3.63
Lawyer	0.50	2.9	5.80
Clergyman	0.39	11.1	28.46
Elementary-secondary teacher	0.16	3.8	23.75
College faculty	0.74	4.1	5.54
Other professions	2.46	4.1	1.67
Total	5.51	30.7	5.57

*U.S. Male Adult Population, 1940, Bureau of the Census, Vol. 1, pp. 75–80.

data were not organized to permit such comparisons. If each institutional type was taken separately, there would be differences, especially among Catholic institution presidents; in this category the professions were not as important sources of leadership, yet there still might have been a more favorable comparison to the general population. Also, the clergyman category was found important for some types of colleges and not others. Almost one-third of all college and university presidents had fathers in professional fields, and the professional category was, in general, the single most important supplier of academic presidents.

Comparisons of Origins

There seem to be more similarities than differences in occupational origins of the various college and university presidents. In fact, when one considers groups that are most similar, it is not so much a question of the *complexity* of the institution, that is, whether it be a college or university, but rather, of the *form of control* of the institution. Thus, the public university and college presidents as a group look very similar, as do the Catholic university and college presidents, the Protestant-related university and college presidents, or the private, independent university and college presidents. There is evidence that social influences and forces in the presidents' backgrounds have played prominent roles in their selection of the institutions where they were educated, where they taught, and where they became president.

Comparisons of the rank orders of occupational groups show that after professional fields, these three categories are in close representation: foremen, government service, business executives, managers, and proprietors. There is evidence that high business positions have not been critical as sources of higher education leadership. The general avenue of higher education tended to be used as a means of upward mobility by those whose fathers were in minor executive positions. Fathers who occupied high status business positions are found among academic presidents, but to a lesser degree—suggesting, therefore, that movement to higher education might not have been the most attractive career goal for the sons of major or large business leaders.

Among college and university presidents, the sons of skilled laborers and farmers (although at a proportional disadvantage) have had career opportunities in higher education administration, and many chose this route for upward mobility. Although the unskilled workers and white-collar workers are far down the line, it is clear that a career in higher education was not closed to the sons of these workers. This is even more clearly seen when the occupational origins of Catholic college presidents are examined.

The occupational origins for all academic presidents in the sample are shown in Table 6, which also includes the percentages of occupational groups represented by the presidents' fathers and the ratios

TABLE 6
OCCUPATIONAL ORIGINS OF ACADEMIC PRESIDENTS

Father's Occupation	Percentage of Presidents	Proportional Representation Ratio
Unskilled, semiskilled laborer	6	0.19
Skilled laborer	10	0.71
Clerk, Salesman	5	0.38
Foreman	7	2.50
Executive, manager, proprietor	21	2.10
Professional	31	6.20
Farmer	16	0.73
Government	3	3.00
Military	1	1.00
Total per cent	100	

formed when comparisons were made with the 1940 census population.

Geographical Origins

Americans have long held firm ideas related to the importance of local, state, and regional ties in their daily lives. Loyalty to and identification with a particular geographical region or community have had an often profound, although subtle, effect on the development of views or life styles of the residents. The Warner studies researched this phenomenon as it related to the territorial origins of business and government executives in order to determine the extent to which certain regions or communities seemed to be associated with the number of individuals reaching executive positions. Did a region supply a proportionally higher number to business and government elite positions than would be expected on the basis of that region's percentage of population in the society? It was found that territorial origins as well as occupational origins played a part in the pattern of mobility of these executives.

When studying the impact of higher education in the United States, one can hardly overlook the fact that state and regional concerns are important. For example, many institutions, especially public colleges and universities, formally state as an objective not only the production, dissemination, and preservation of truth, but also service to the people of the state, in the sense of educational and financial assistance programs in centers throughout the state. Furthermore, it is common for some state legislatures to hassle over whether out-of-state enrollments should be held down to a given proportion or even if certain states (for a variety of reasons) should have restricted enrollments.

On the other hand, the private colleges and universities tend to select more upon a national, regional, or religious basis for students and often for faculty as well. Some institutions take great pride in the fact that the faculty and staff represent many regions of the country and world and thereby promote a more cosmopolitan educational climate. Others indicate a preference to build upon local talents and recruit those who are assumed to be sensitive to the needs of the people in the area. It is clear that some states and regions provide what appear to be large numbers of private and public institutions of higher education while others provide few, sometimes reflecting population needs and sometimes not. Thus, there is reason to investigate the geographical origins of the academic presidents to determine if there is some relation between their origins and career mobility. Do these academic presidents originate randomly—that is, as would be expected, on the basis of population or the number of colleges and universities found in a given region? What can be learned of the broad streams of physical mobility of these educators across the country, using data on their birthplaces and the locations of their present positions? Do any regions seem to be at an advantage in retaining educators at the expense of other regions?

The academic presidents were asked whether they were born in the United States and, if so, in which state. By turning to federal census data for population statistics, it is possible to relate the population data to the presidents' birthplaces to learn if some regions or communities produced more college and university presidents than others. Since the presidents were born, on the average, around 1915, it was decided to use census data for 1920 as a reasonable estimate of the distribution of the national population at the time the presidents were born. Federal census data divide the United States into nine census regions; the same regional classification is used in this study and is as follows:

New England: Maine, Vermont, New Hampshire, Massachusetts, Connecticut, and Rhode Island.

Middle Atlantic: New York, Pennsylvania, and New Jersey.

South Atlantic: Delaware, Maryland, West Virginia, Virginia, North Carolina, South Carolina, Georgia, and Florida.

East North Central: Wisconsin, Michigan, Illinois, Indiana, and Ohio.

East South Central: Kentucky, Tennessee, Alabama, and Mississippi.

West North Central: Minnesota, North Dakota, South Dakota, Iowa, Nebraska, Kansas, and Missouri.

West South Central: Oklahoma, Arkansas, Louisiana, and Texas.

Mountain: Montana, Idaho, Wyoming, Nevada, Utah, Colorado, Arizona, and New Mexico.

Pacific: Washington, Oregon, and California; (plus Hawaii and Alaska).

Table 7 shows the percentages of academic presidents born in

TABLE 7

DISTRIBUTION OF UNITED STATES-BORN ACADEMIC PRESIDENTS

Region	Percentage of Presidents Born in Region	Percentage of Population (1920)* Living in Region	Proportional Representation Ratio
New England	7.3	7.0	1.04
Middle Atlantic	18.4	21.1	0.87
South Atlantic	12.3	13.2	0.93
East South Central	8.1	8.4	0.96
West South Central	9.4	9.7	0.97
East North Central	21.2	20.3	1.04
West North Central	16.1	11.9	1.35
Mountain	2.9	3.1	0.94
Pacific	4.3	5.3	0.81
Total per cent	100.0	100.0	
Total number of presidents:		716	

*Bureau of the Census, 1920, Vol. 1.

each census region, along with the respective ratios—computed in the same manner as those for occupational origins—that more exactly show the extent that specific regions have "produced" academic presidents. (In order to insure anonymity of all respondents, results are given for all academic presidents in each region rather than by institutional types.)

States in the East North Central (21.2 per cent) and Middle Atlantic regions (18.4 per cent) produced the greatest percentage of college and university presidents. And in these regions, only three states had supplied 170 (nearly 24 per cent) of the college and university presidents in the total sample: sixty-three presidents were born in Pennsylvania (which gave the most in the nation); fifty-six were born in New York; and fifty-one were born in Illinois. However, if one considers only the ratios in the far right column of Table 7, then it is apparent that only three regions supplied a percentage of academic presidents that were greater than their proportion in the United States population would suggest. The New England, East North Central, and West North Central states gave in greater proportions, but only the West North Central stands out among the three as giving an appreciable percentage more than their population percentage, with a ratio of 1.35.[3]

3. The reader is cautioned that the figure might be biased upward somewhat since a higher proportion of respondents from the West North Central region are in the study

No region stands out very high or very low in terms of the percentage of presidents supplied, and six of the nine regions have ratios within 0.07 of a perfect representation indicated by 1.00. The data suggest that college and university presidents came from a close representation of the general population at the time they were born, and only one region (West North Central) had produced what could be regarded as a relatively higher proportion of academic presidents.

The argument can reasonably be made that certain regions have more colleges and universities than others, thus creating more professional opportunities for educational leadership that retain and attract individuals across state and region boundaries. This fact might account for some of the variance and for the relatively high percentage in the West North Central region, regardless of the percentages in the sample. Therefore, rather than using census data, ratios should be developed based upon the percentage of colleges and universities in each region. This adjustment would offer a more complete picture of the impact of territorial origins by interjecting a notion of professional opportunities as well. Table 8 presents a summary of this analysis.[4]

By developing a different approach to geographical origins, it is clear that three regions lead all others in the sheer number of four-year colleges and universities that have needed and attracted (from within and without) academic presidents over a period of time. The Middle Atlantic states have 16.7 per cent of all four-year institutions, the East North Central states have 15.7 per cent, and the South Atlantic states have 15.6 per cent of all such institutions. The states that lead all others in the nation for four-year institutions are: New York with eighty-eight, Pennsylvania with seventy-eight, California with seventy, Massachusetts with forty-nine, Ohio with forty-eight, Texas with forty-seven, and Illinois with forty-four.

When one examines the ratios that were based upon the percentage of institutions available rather than national population statistics, a far different pattern emerges. The West North Central states still retain a high rank among all regions, but the neighboring states

than one would expect by chance. Although the West North Central region has 12.6 per cent of all four-year colleges and universities, some 15.4 per cent of the presidents in the study sample are from that region.

4. The percentages given for colleges and universities were based upon the 1,118 four-year institutions that served as the population for the study, and not simply the 760 institutions represented by the respondents. The latter figure might have seriously biased the results.

TABLE 8
DISTRIBUTION OF COLLEGE PRESIDENTS IN NINE CENSUS REGIONS

Region	Percentage of Presidents Born in Region	Percentage of All Four-Year Colleges in Region	Proportional Representation Ratio From Region
New England	7.3	8.9	0.82
Middle Atlantic	18.4	16.7	1.10
South Atlantic	12.3	15.6	0.79
East South Central	8.1	7.8	1.04
West South Central	9.4	8.8	1.07
East North Central	21.2	15.7	1.35
West North Central	16.1	12.6	1.28
Mountain	2.9	4.3	0.67
Pacific	4.3	9.6	0.45
Total per cent	100.0	100.0	

Total number of presidents: 716
Total number of colleges and universities: 1,118

in the East North Central region move a little ahead with a ratio of 1.35.[5]

The Middle Atlantic, East South Central, and West South Central states have a better representation while the Mountain and Pacific regions are definitely low with respective ratios of 0.67 and 0.45. This would indicate: (1) these latter two regions at least had drawn upon a fair percentage of educational leaders born outside the regions to head their colleges and universities, and (2) such educators had found the opportunities in the Mountain and Pacific regions attractive enough to move in that direction.

Indications are that our chief higher educational leaders came from all regions of the country in a fair representation of the general population, and no single region decisively seemed to provide any advantages over another. However, the presidents in their careers have been mobile between regions. When the percentages of four-year institutions in each region are considered, there is evidence that academic presidents have been men in geographic motion, similar to their counterparts in business and government. Some regions such

5. Again the reader is cautioned to review the data given in Appendix A on the exact percentages of colleges by regions that are a little under- or overrepresented in the sample. Whereas the institutions in the Middle Atlantic and South Atlantic regions were somewhat underrepresented in the sample, the East North Central and West North Central regions were somewhat overrepresented.

as the East North Central, West North Central, and Middle Atlantic seem to have produced not only enough presidents for their own institutions, but for others as well. The Mountain, Pacific, and New England regions, on the other hand, seemed to provide professional opportunities, based on their relatively larger numbers of institutions, to draw upon educators born in other regions. (The attractability of the Pacific region has been underscored as well by the great growth of the area in population and higher education over the past sixty years.)

Urban and Rural Origins

It has been noted that not only states and regions provide loyalties and often-shared experiences to individuals, but also that the types and sizes of communities where individuals are born provide such basic experiences. With this in mind, the research investigated sizes and types of communities of the academic presidents' birthplaces. Are these men representative of American society in terms of the communities where they were born and presumably reared? That is, to what extent were they big city boys, small town boys, farm boys? To assist in this analysis, 1920 census data were used to determine how representative the birthplaces were. Tables 9 and 10 summarize the findings, in percentages, for university and college presidents, respectively, and Table 11 gives the results in ratio form for more exact comparisons.

On the basis of the percentages and ratios found in these tables

TABLE 9
UNIVERSITY PRESIDENTS: SIZE OF BIRTHPLACE

Size of Community	Percentage of U.S. Population[a]	Percentage of Presidents				All Presidents
		Public	Catholic	Protestant	Independent	
Rural or less than 2,500	48	50	0	52	28	40
2,500 to 25,000	16	15	20	19	20	18
25,000 to 100,000	10	12	10	10	17	12
Over 100,000	26	23	70	19	35	30
Total per cent	100	100	100	100	100	100
Total number of presidents:	161					

[a]Bureau of the Census, 1920, Vol. 1, p. 50.

TABLE 10

LIBERAL ARTS PRESIDENTS: SIZE OF BIRTHPLACE

Size of Community	Percentage of U.S. Population	Percentage of Presidents					All Presidents
		Public	Cath.	Prot.	Indep.	Techn.	
Rural or less than 2,500	48	57	21	44	28	41	40
2,500 to 25,000	16	18	14	25	25	17	20
25,000 to 100,000	10	13	25	14	20	10	17
Over 100,000	26	12	40	17	27	32	23
Total per cent	100	100	100	100	100	100	100
Total number of presidents: 591							

there seem to be varied patterns of the types and sizes of American communities represented by the college and university presidents. About 40 per cent of all academic presidents were born in rural communities of less than 2,500 population giving a ratio of 0.83, or somewhat under what one could expect on the basis of the general population at that time. It should be noted, however, that there are variations which seem to be associated with the presidents' type of institution. For example, presidents of public colleges and universities and private Protestant-related colleges and universities were fairly representative of 1920 America, whereas Catholic college and university presidents clearly were born in urban communities; to a lesser degree the same can be said for the presidents of the private, independent liberal arts colleges and universities.

When the small town origins of 2,500 to 25,000 population size are considered, it is found that the presidents across the board are fairly representative of these communities. In the cities of 25,000 to

TABLE 11

RATIO OF SIZE OF BIRTHPLACE OF ACADEMIC PRESIDENTS AND
SIZE OF RESIDENCE OF U.S. POPULATION

Size of Community	University Presidents				Liberal Arts College Presidents					All Presidents*
	Public	Cath.	Prot.	Indep.	Public	Cath.	Prot.	Indep.	Tech.	
Rural or less than 2,500	1.04	0.00	1.08	0.58	1.18	0.44	0.92	0.58	0.85	0.83
2,500 to 25,000	0.94	1.25	1.19	1.25	1.13	0.88	1.56	1.56	1.06	1.19
25,000–100,000	1.20	1.00	1.00	1.70	1.30	2.50	1.40	2.00	1.00	1.60
Over 100,000	0.88	2.69	0.73	1.35	0.46	1.54	0.65	1.04	1.23	0.92

*Note: This information is based upon analysis of Tables 9 and 10.

100,000 residents, there is nearly a 60 per cent overrepresentation. While 10 per cent of the population were in these larger cities, nearly 16 per cent of the presidents were born there. In the large cities of over 100,000 people—which comprised 26 per cent of the population—some 24 per cent of all presidents are represented. However, again there are important variations depending upon the presidents' institutions. For example, 70 per cent of the Catholic university presidents and 40 per cent of the Catholic college presidents come from large urban communities while there is a drastic drop in the relative percentage of public liberal arts presidents born in large urban areas.

It can be said that the heads of public colleges and universities and Protestant-related colleges and universities are well-representative of the general population in coming from rural communities and smaller urban settings, while these presidents tend not to come from large metropolitan cities. On the other hand, Catholic institution presidents are definitely of urban geographical origins with a majority from the larger cities.

A relatively small number of academic presidents were born and raised outside the United States. Only thirty-three college and university presidents (or about 4 per cent, and nearly all men) were foreign-born, and they were found in all types of institutions.

5

Family Influences

The Warner executive studies indicated that a father's occupation influences the son, not only by giving the child a particular status in the community, but also by providing him with particular role models and opportunities for social mobility. This idea prompts an analysis of occupational mobility beginning with the paternal and maternal grandfathers and moving in succession to the fathers of academic presidents. In addition, a survey of the occupations of the wives' fathers is conducted to determine if the presidents married up, down, or across in an occupational sense, and thereby learn how marriage might be related to their career mobility.

Paternal Grandfathers

Among all university presidents, except those heading Catholic universities, we find that there is a definite movement away from farming occupations when the careers of their grandfathers and fathers are contrasted. The primary movement is from farming to professional fields and to minor and major positions in the business

TABLE 12

OCCUPATIONS OF PATERNAL GRANDFATHERS AND FATHERS OF ACADEMIC PRESIDENTS

	Percentage of Presidents									
	Public		Catholic		Prot.-Related		Independent		Technical	
Occupation	P.G.[1]	F.[2]	P.G.	F.	P.G.	F.	P.G.	F.	P.G.	F.
A. University Presidents										
Unskilled laborer	5	2	0	10	0	5	0	3		
Skilled laborer	8	8	33	10	0	5	15	0		
Clerk, sales	0	0	0	10	6	5	4	7		
Foreman	4	7	17	15	6	5	0	14		
Major executive	1	7	6	20	0	5	0	10		
Small business owner	8	13	28	5	22	5	12	0		
Large business owner	1	3	6	15	0	0	0	14		
Professional	21	32	6	10	11	40	34	45		
Farmer	42	20	6	0	56	30	31	7		
Government	10	6	0	5	0	0	4	0		
Military	0	1	0	0	0	0	0	0		
Total per cent	100	100*	100*	100	100*	100	100	100		
B. Liberal Arts Presidents										
Unskilled laborer	10	4	17	14	8	6	5	6	5	3
Skilled laborer	15	13	20	14	9	10	11	4	5	3
Clerk, sales	1	4	2	9	2	4	0	1	0	7
Foreman	0	4	3	12	1	6	3	3	5	7
Major executive	2	6	3	6	1	6	6	10	0	0
Small business owner	12	14	9	13	8	9	11	8	10	13
Large business owner	1	3	0	2	0	1	2	4	0	4
Professional	8	24	7	13	17	39	23	48	17	25
Farmer	49	21	39	10	50	17	33	11	49	25
Government	2	6	1	5	2	3	6	4	9	3
Military	0	1	0	2	2	1	0	1	0	10
Total per cent	100	100	100*	100	100	100*	100	100	100	100

[1] Paternal Grandfathers

[2] Fathers

*Does not total 100 percent exactly due to rounding of figures.

hierarchy. The comparisons of the occupations of the paternal grandfathers and fathers are shown in Table 12.

A review of the grandfathers' occupations shows that few were in the laborer categories, except for the grandfathers of Catholic university presidents, one-third of whom were skilled workers. The Catholic university presidents have occupational origins in the business sector that continue back through the second generation to the third generation. The fact observed earlier that Catholic university presidents have quite different occupational origins from other presidents extends back to the grandparents. For the public, Protestant-related, and independent university presidents, the intergenerational occupational succession emanated largely from a farming and professional base of the grandfathers.

The roots of occupational mobility extend back to the late 1800s, and it is evident that no occupational group was frozen from one generation to the other. In the occupational movement over the generations there appears to have been an inculcation of the value of education and of achieving that undoubtedly had many direct and subtle effects on some university presidents' career goals. More convincing support for the idea of probable influences between generations is clearer in the case of private, independent university presidents where one-third of their grandfathers were professional men.

The occupational origins of liberal arts presidents beginning with the paternal grandfathers show a general transition from the farm to the city, similar to the sketch of the university presidents. Among presidents of non-Catholic colleges, the movement is definitely from the farms to the colleges where a large percentage of fathers prepared for professional careers. Complementing this mobility is the general upward rise in the business hierarchy of the grandfathers who were found in the laborer classes to their sons who achieved higher level executive positions.

In Table 13, comparisons are offered for the occupations of the paternal grandfathers and fathers of all academic presidents. An occupational breakdown of the paternal grandfathers and fathers of all presidents tells much of the story of continuity of occupations from grandfather to father to son. The prominence of professional and farming occupational origins of academic presidents is more clearly in evidence.

Although there are differences in the occupational origins of different groupings of academic presidents, about 43 per cent of the grandfathers engaged in farming. Second in rank order were the lower level business occupations, primarily unskilled and skilled laborers (22 per cent), and third were professional men (15 per cent). Another 16 per cent were comprised of combined categories of business executives (5 per cent) and business owners (11 per cent). In the next generation, or among the fathers of academic presidents, the farming occupational base is sharply reduced, and there is a

TABLE 13
SUMMARY OF OCCUPATIONS

Occupations	Percentage of Grandfathers	Percentage of Fathers
Professions	15	31
Physician	2	2
Engineer	1	3
Lawyer	2	3
Clergyman	6	11
Elementary-secondary teacher	1	4
College faculty	2	4
Other professions	1	4
Farming	43	16
Laborers, clerks, sales	22	21
Business executives	5	13
Business owners	11	14
Other occupations	4	5
Total per cent	100	100

doubling of those in professional fields (31 per cent). Although all professions show increases between the father's father and the father, the percentage increases in the clergy and secondary and higher education are most evident. The category of laborers and white collar workers stayed about the same, but a larger percentage of fathers moved up to skilled workers and white collar workers while only 6 per cent of the 21 per cent represented unskilled laborers, the remaining being skilled. The combined categories of business executive and business owner grew from 16 per cent to 27 per cent as there were fairly proportional increases in foremen, major business executives, small business owners, and large business owners among the fathers.

An examination of the occupational origins of all college and university presidents reveals that a majority of their fathers and grandfathers were United States-born. About two-thirds of the paternal grandfathers and 85 per cent of the fathers were born in the United States. The only significant variation in these percentages is found among the Catholic college and university presidents; about 80 per cent of their fathers but only about one-third of their paternal grandfathers were born in the United States. In all cases, the fathers and grandfathers of the private, independent college presidents represent the largest percentage born in the United States, as 93 per cent of the fathers and 81 per cent of the grandfathers were United States-born.

It would appear that the professional and farming occupational origins for many of the non-Catholic institution presidents are tied to the fact that their families have been in the country well back into the rural-oriented America of the 1800s and have had a longer period of time to rise up through professional and business leadership. The Catholic institution presidents, on the other hand, primarily represent only the second generation born in this country and their rapid mobility stems from urban centers up through the business sector into religious life culminating in higher educational leadership.

Maternal Grandfathers

Sociologists and anthropologists have often studied occupational succession through the mother's lineage, in addition to the father's lineage, as a significant aspect of the interstructural connections of family and occupational status in this society.[1] Such an investigation was conducted with the academic presidents to obtain a more complete perspective of the probable family influences on the presidents' careers. An analysis of the mother's father's occupation shows: (1) the status of the mother when the president's father married her and how different or similar their statuses were, and (2) other probable influences translated from mother to son in the form of values and career goals that resulted from her own earlier family life.

The occupational levels of the presidents' maternal and paternal grandfathers are quite similar in most categories, as shown in Table 14. In the professional, farming, and lower-level business occupations, there are very similar occupational origins reflected by the maternal and paternal grandfathers. In an anthropological sense, there is evidence of endogamy, that is, marriages at the same occupational level. Slightly more of the maternal grandfathers than paternal grandfathers are found in the business executive category, and in the business owner category, and about 4 per cent more of the

1. See for example, W. Lloyd Warner and others, *The American Federal Executive* (Yale University Press, 1963), Chapter 6, pp. 84–89.

TABLE 14

OCCUPATIONS OF GRANDFATHERS OF COLLEGE PRESIDENTS

Occupations	Percentage of:	
	Father's Father	Mother's Father
Professions	**15**	**15**
Physician	2	1
Engineer	1	1
Lawyer	2	2
Clergyman	6	5
Elementary-secondary teacher	1	2
College faculty	2	2
Other professions	1	2
Farming	**43**	**40**
Laborers, white-collar	**22**	**21**
Business executives	**5**	**7**
Business owners	**11**	**15**
Other occupations	**4**	**2**
Total per cent	100	100

mother's fathers were small business entrepreneurs. For neither grandparents is there a strong indication of involvement in education as such, even though the professions are strongly represented. In general, it can be said that the presidents' occupational origins as reflected in the occupations of their paternal and maternal grandfathers are at about the same levels, with a slightly greater percentage of maternal grandfathers in higher levels of the business hierarchy than the paternal grandfathers.

The analysis shows that the president's mother and father tended to marry at the same status level; this suggests that they undoubtedly reinforced certain values toward success and mobility among their sons. The presidents' fathers made their ways into colleges and universities and entered the professions in twice the proportion as the grandparents.

In a more detailed analysis of the grandfathers' occupations based on the grouping of presidents of different institutions, no significant deviations were found. It has been noted that two-thirds of the paternal grandfathers were born in the United States, except for those grandfathers of Catholic institution presidents, and about two-thirds of the maternal grandparents were also United States-born. As would be expected, only 30 per cent of the maternal grandparents of Catholic college presidents were United States-born. As in the case of the birthplaces of the academic presidents' fathers, about 85 per cent of the mothers were born in the United States.

The study examined how much education was actually received by the parents of academic presidents. Judging from the occupations of the fathers it might be expected that many of them would be college graduates, however, about 45 per cent of the fathers and

TABLE 15
EDUCATION OF PARENTS OF COLLEGE PRESIDENTS

Highest Educational Level Attained	Percentage of:	
	Fathers	Mothers
Less than high school	33	31
Some high school	12	12
High school graduate	13	24
Some college	14	18
College graduate	10	14
Post-graduate study	17	2
Total per cent	100*	100*

*Does not total 100 per cent exactly due to rounding of figures.

mothers of these top educators received less than a high school education. Of the approximately 54 per cent of the fathers and mothers who graduated from high school, one-half of the number of fathers went on to graduate from college while about one-fourth of the mothers graduated from college. Twenty-four per cent of the mothers terminated their formal education at the end of high school. However, it can be seen that 18 per cent of the mothers did obtain some college work and probably many met their spouses in college. It is not surprising that such a large percentage of the fathers received undergraduate and advanced degrees since it has been observed that 31 per cent of the fathers were in the professions, almost all of which require a college education. More than 25 per cent of the mothers' fathers were either professional men or business leaders, many of whom had the opportunity to give financial assistance, knowledge, and encouragement to their daughters to attend college.

Such forces were linked to the largely endogamic relationships that characterized the presidents' parents' marriages, and unquestionably played a role in reinforcing, advising, and maybe even insisting that their sons pursue college degrees in preparation for a professional career. Although about one-third of the parents did not receive a high school diploma, the child undoubtedly had or identified with certain role-models and values that prized education. A significant percentage of the presidents, however, were raised in homes where their fathers and mothers were college-educated and almost one-fifth of the fathers pursued college work beyond the bachelor's degree. The models and values related to the value of education in these latter families often extended into the third generation having direct and indirect effects on the grandsons. Since the study of occupational succession of all academic presidents through the third generation shows a profile of primarily occupationally mobile families, the non-college educated parents, although at the lower occupational levels, presumably saw education as a road to a better life for their sons and daughters and supported this direction rather than using means to keep the sons at their own lower occupational levels.

Through each generation, beginning with the grandfathers of the presidents, there is evidence of upward mobility and a continual succession of growing professional and business leadership proportions, and a continual decrease in the percentages in rural or urban, lower level, business positions. This mobility trend has culminated with the sons who are the subjects of this research, the presidents of a majority of American colleges and universities.

Wives of Academic Presidents

Less than 2 per cent of all the presidents of non-Catholic institutions are single, while nearly all presidents are married and have, on the average, three children. The question of whether the presidents tended to marry at higher, similar, or lower occupational levels might now be raised. Was the general pattern of endogamy that was found among their parents repeated in their own lives? Since their wives' ascribed statuses immediately prior to marriage came from their fathers' occupations, a comparison was made of the occupations of the academic presidents' fathers with those of the wives' fathers.

In general, there is a fair amount of similarity in the occupational levels of the non-Catholic university president's father and the wife's father, although there are greater differences than existed

TABLE 16

OCCUPATIONAL ORIGINS

	Percentage of Non-Catholic Institution:	
Occupations	Presidents' Fathers	Wives' Fathers
Professions	36	27
Physician	2	4
Engineer	3	3
Lawyer	3	3
Clergyman	14	6
Elementary-secondary teachers	5	3
College faculty	5	5
Other professions	4	3
Farming	18	15
Laborers, white-collar	17	16
Business executives	12	15
Business owners	13	20
Other occupations	4	7
Total per cent	100	100

between the presidents' paternal and maternal grandfathers. On the one hand, a much greater percentage of presidents' fathers came from professional fields than did the wives' fathers. About 36 per cent of the presidents' fathers were professional men (with 14 per cent as clergymen), while only 27 per cent of the wives' fathers were professionals (and only 6 per cent as clergymen), as shown in Table 16.

Within the farming occupations, the presidents' fathers were found in somewhat larger proportions than were the wives' fathers. Within the business occupations, fewer of the wives' fathers were laborers or white-collar workers when compared to the presidents' fathers, but a larger percentage of wives' fathers were in major business executive positions (10 per cent), and a larger percentage were owners of large businesses (7 per cent) than was found with the presidents' fathers. There is, then, evidence of a fair amount of endogamy between the presidents and their wives at the time of their marriages, with some important variations.

An analysis of the occupations of the wives' fathers supports the fact that the women represent, on the average, higher occupational origins than those represented by the presidents' mothers. About 45 per cent of the wives' fathers were either professional men, major business executives, or large business owners. It could be expected that the wives (as in the case of the presidents' mothers) were given opportunities for higher education and social opportunities to meet men who were highly mobile themselves. In short, the women the presidents married have occupational origins somewhat similar to their own and considerably higher than the mothers' statuses at their time of marriage.

Among academic presidents, occupational mobility continued and is reflected in their marriages. Among certain groups within the society, there is the notion, no matter how ill-founded, that marrying the boss's daughter provides leverage to top positions for many men, and some might believe this to be true in higher education administration. However, there is certainly no real evidence for this "myth" among academic presidents. In fact only eight of the total number of academic presidents in the study married women whose fathers were college presidents.

6

Educational Backgrounds

Education is instrumental in preparing individuals for high levels of responsibility, and also in providing a critical avenue to leadership positions in American society. Studies of government and business executives have found that education, particularly at the college level, helped prepare these men for their roles, and such education presented opportunities to those born of lower occupational origins to rise into elite positions. It would seem only reasonable to expect that the heads of American colleges and universities would be well-educated persons, with most having earned advanced graduate degrees. In this study, a number of questions were asked about the academic presidents' formal educational preparation. For example: What was the extent of their formal education and the highest degree earned? How many had earned the academic doctorate or other degrees? What was the nature of their education including the major fields of study? Where and in what types of institutions did they receive their education? How many presidents were students at the institutions they now head?

Academic presidents are a very well-educated group of men and women, and a majority of them have earned advanced degrees.

When one considers all college and university presidents as a single group, the data show that nearly three-fourths have earned an academic doctorate; 16 per cent have a master's degree, 6 per cent have earned a professional graduate degree, and 5 per cent have a bachelor's degree. As shown in Table 17, the doctor of philosophy degree leads all doctorates with 58 percent, while 11 per cent have earned the doctor of education degree, 1 per cent, the doctor of sacred theology (the academic doctorate for theological study earned by Roman Catholic priests), and 3 per cent have earned other academic doctorates.

Among the presidents of major institutional types, the presidents of public liberal arts colleges represent the largest percentage who have earned an academic doctorate, as nine out of ten are so educated. Public university presidents follow with 78 per cent having earned the doctorate, while most other institutional types have close to 75 per cent with a doctorate. It can be seen that only the presidents of the Protestant-related universities and liberal arts colleges have a relatively smaller percentage who have earned a doctorate (66 per cent and 61 per cent, respectively).

A closer examination of those who have earned the doctorate reveals that the degree earned by most is doctor of philosophy how-

TABLE 17
HIGHEST ACADEMIC DEGREE EARNED BY ACADEMIC PRESIDENTS

Highest Degree Earned	Percentage of Presidents
Bachelor's degree	5
Master's degree	16
Doctoral degree	73
Doctor of Philosophy	58
Doctor of Education	11
Doctor of Sacred Theology	1
Other Academic Doctorate	3
Other graduate degrees	6
Medicine	0.5
Law	2
Divinity	3
Other religious degrees	0.5
Total per cent	100.0
Total number of presidents: 760	

TABLE 18

A COMPARISON OF ACADEMIC DEGREES EARNED

Highest Degree Earned	Percentage of University Presidents				Percentage of Liberal Arts Presidents				
	Public	Cath.	Prot.	Indep.	Public	Cath.	Prot.	Indep.	Techn.
Bachelor's	6	5	0	0	1	5	6	7	20
Master's	8	15	19	17	7	23	21	15	10
Doctorate	78	75	66	76	91	70	61	73	70
Philosophy	68	55	66	72	51	64	51	67	61
Education	9	0	0	0	37	2	5	5	3
Sacred Theology	0	20	0	0	0	3	0	0	0
Other	1	0	0	4	3	1	5	1	6
Other graduate degrees	8	5	15	7	1	2	12	5	0
Medicine	3	0	0	0	0	0	0	1	0
Law	3	0	5	7	1	0	2	3	0
Divinity	2	0	5	0	0	0	9	1	0
Other religious	0	5	5	0	0	2	1	0	0
Total per cent	100	100	100	100	100	100	100	100	100

ever, the doctor of education degree was earned by 37 per cent of the public liberal arts college presidents. About 9 per cent of public university presidents have also earned the doctor of education degree. Among Catholic educators, the doctor of sacred theology was a prominent program of study along with the doctor of philosophy degree.

An analysis of the degrees earned shows that the bachelor of divinity curriculum—the usual degree for Protestant clergymen— was completed by a fairly large percentage, especially among those who head Protestant-related universities and colleges. It is evident that few presidents were specifically and formally trained to be medical doctors or lawyers.

Of the average of 16 per cent of all presidents who earned a degree no higher than the master's level, there are again variations based upon the president's type of institution. The differences are more noticeable among presidents of private institutions: Catholic liberal arts presidents (23 per cent), Protestant-related college presidents (21 per cent), and Protestant-related university presidents (19 per cent). Those presidents who had earned bachelors' degrees and no higher are found in relatively few numbers within each major type of institution, although there is a slightly larger percentage in public universities and private liberal arts colleges.

The only difference in the extent of higher education of male and female presidents is that a relatively greater percentage of men have received a bachelor's degree as the highest degree while a relatively higher percentage of women have earned the master's and doctoral degrees. This is shown in Table 19.

TABLE 19
HIGHEST DEGREE EARNED BY MEN AND BY WOMEN

Highest Degree Earned	Percentage of Men	Percentage of Women
Bachelor's	6	1
Master's	15	20
Academic doctorate	72	75
Other degrees	7	4
Total per cent	100	100

When the extent of education of presidents of institutions in different regions of the country was considered, there were only minor differences, as seen in Table 20. Institutions in New England seem to have a relatively larger percentage of presidents who earned a master's degree and no higher, but it is also true that a larger number of Catholic liberal arts colleges and Protestant-related colleges and universities are found in New England, and a good percentage of these presidents possess the master's and no higher. The same explanation holds for the relatively high percentage of presidents with no higher than a master's degree in the East North Central

TABLE 20
REGIONAL DISTRIBUTION OF DEGREES

Region of President's Institution	Highest Degree Earned, in Percentages				
	B.A.	M.A.	Ph.D.	Other	Total
New England	6	22	67	5	100
Middle Atlantic	6	13	77	4	100
South Atlantic	9	12	68	11	100
East South Central	0	17	76	7	100
West South Central	5	15	72	8	100
East North Central	3	21	70	6	100
West North Central	7	11	74	8	100
Mountain	3	11	80	6	100
Pacific	4	18	77	1	100

region. In the South Atlantic region, there is a large percentage of Protestant-related colleges and this largely accounts for the somewhat greater "other degrees" earned since many of these presidents earned bachelor of divinity degrees.

Programs of Study

The academic presidents indicated their fields of study—undergraduate and graduate—in addition to their highest degrees attained. These fields of study were categorized into five major groups: (1) *applied fields* (including the study of agriculture, business disciplines, and engineering curricula); (2) *education* (including elementary and secondary education, educational administration, and guidance); (3) *natural sciences* (including the physical, biological, and mathematical sciences); (4) *humanities* (including philosophy, history, religion, literature, and the classics); and (5) *social sciences* (including sociology, anthropology, psychology, economics, and political science). The fields of study for presidents of all types of institutions at the following four distinct degree levels were examined: (1) undergraduate or bachelor's, (2) master's, (3) doctorate, and (4) other professional degree level.

While academic presidents studied nearly all curricula, they indicated an emphasis in some fields of study more often than others. Distribution of the five major programs of study for all presidents at the undergraduate level is shown in Table 21. Among all academic presidents, nearly one-half took undergraduate degrees in the

TABLE 21

FIELDS OF STUDY OF ACADEMIC PRESIDENTS

Program of Study	Percentage of Presidents' Programs at		
	Undergraduate Level n = 760	Master's Level n = 590	Doctoral Level n = 552
Applied fields	12.1	9.3	6.9
Education	7.3	26.8	29.7
Natural sciences	17.8	10.7	12.7
Humanities	49.3	39.5	36.8
Social sciences	13.5	13.7	13.9
Total per cent	100.0	100.0	100.0

humanities or general arts and letters fields. For those presidents who head technological institutions, combinations of engineering and the physical-mathematical sciences were listed as the most prevalent undergraduate majors (64 per cent). The humanities tended to be the most popular programs especially for all the private college and university presidents with about 60 per cent of these presidents having earned an undergraduate degree in these related disciplines. Only the public university and public liberal arts college presidents earned a relatively large percentage of bachelor's degrees in disciplines outside the humanities, mainly education and social science. Nevertheless, the humanities still ranked first among the presidents of public institutions.

A majority of the academic presidents majored in humanities, that is, the fields most often regarded as central to the liberal education and preparatory to the professions. The natural sciences, applied fields, and social sciences were also prominent educational programs. Secondary education was pursued by a small percentage of the individuals, and most of them now head public liberal arts colleges.

At the master's degree level, the humanities were still the most important fields of study for academic presidents, but there was some movement to other disciplines as well. It can be seen in Table 21 that the humanities were quite popular, but there is a 10 per cent reduction when compared to undergraduate programs studied. Also reduced in percentages from the bachelor's to master's levels are the applied fields (from 12.1 per cent to 9.3 per cent) and the natural sciences (from 17.8 per cent to 10.7 per cent). The program of study reflecting the greatest increase was education. While only 7.3 per cent earned undergraduate degrees in education, over 26 per cent earned master's degrees in education. It would appear that at the conclusion of their undergraduate programs a relatively large percentage shifted from the humanities, natural sciences, and applied fields to the general field of education.

The general movement to education occured among those who now head all types of institutions but the movement was greatest among the heads of public liberal arts colleges where nearly one-half earned master's degrees in education. Only about 19 per cent of the presidents of other types of institutions earned master's degrees in education. Five hundred and ninety presidents out of the sample of 760—that is, 77.6 per cent, earned master's degrees.

Data showing doctoral level curricula completed by the 72.6 per cent or 552 college and university presidents indicate that the trend away from the humanities continued at the doctoral level but was drastically reduced. Well over one-third of college and university presidents earned academia's highest formal degree, the doctorate, in the humanities disciplines. The percentage taking degrees in the applied fields continued to decline to 6.9 per cent, while there was a slight increase, from 10.7 to 12.7 per cent, in the natural sciences. The percentage in the social sciences continued to stay at about the same rate, increasing very slightly to 13.9 per cent. In the education fields, there was a 3 per cent increase to 29.7 per cent, with some 11 per cent earning an Ed.D. and 18.7 per cent earning a doctor of philosophy degree in education. Analysis based on the type of institution the president now heads shows some variations. For example, nearly 55 per cent of the public liberal arts presidents earned doctorates in education. Among all the presidents of private institutions, about 63 per cent took their doctoral training in the humanities and social sciences.

A relatively large percentage of academic presidents earned degrees other than those in the traditional programs just reviewed. While all the presidents in this study earned at least a bachelor's degree and most moved on to a master's and doctorate, 140 individuals (about 18.6 per cent) earned other types of degrees, as shown in Table 22.

The graduate divinity degree (B.D.) was earned by seventy-four persons, nearly 10 per cent, of the academic presidents in the sample. The vast majority (fifty-six individuals) who have earned the bachelor of divinity degree are now presidents of Protestant-related liberal arts colleges. As such, these degrees mean that about 27 per cent of the presidents of Protestant-related liberal arts colleges are

TABLE 22
OTHER DEGREES EARNED BY ACADEMIC PRESIDENTS

Program of Study	Percentage of Presidents
Medicine	0.4
Law	2.1
Divinity	9.9
Other religious	4.3
Other degrees	1.9
Total per cent	18.6

professionally-educated ministers. Another 19 per cent of the presidents of Protestant-related universities are also professionally-educated ministers who received the bachelor of divinity degree.

The category of other religious degrees represents special programs of study completed mainly by the male presidents of Catholic colleges and universities.

Institutions Attended

It is now pertinent to consider the types of institutions where these men and women received their education. Were they educated primarily in a few colleges and universities at each degree level, or did they receive their formal education randomly at institutions throughout the country? Were private college and university presidents educated mainly in private institutions and were public college and university presidents educated mainly in public institutions? Were most of the presidents educated primarily in a few regions of the country or in many different regions?

It must be kept in mind that there is great diversity between and among American colleges and universities in a number of fundamental respects. Such diversity affects the content and quality of education received by the students of an institution over a period of time. Any attempt to categorize institutions is fraught with difficulties and potential errors since the uniqueness of each is necessarily hidden. A classification scheme such as the institution's form of control reveals general but important patterns and trends.

The examination of the academic presidents' education begins with Table 23—giving an analysis of the types of institutions where the presidents received their degrees. For purposes of clarity, the customary breakdown for the type of institution the president now heads will continue. In addition, the following five general classes show the type of institution where the president received his degree: (1) private liberal arts college, (2) private university, (3) public liberal arts college. (4) public university, and (5) private or public technological institution. The private institutions may have some relationship to a religious body or be independent; the public institutions may be city, state, or federally supported. The formal accreditation of the institution indicated whether it was recognized as a university or college.

In general, the data show that more than one-half of all academic presidents (52 per cent) received their undergraduate degrees in private liberal arts colleges, 17 per cent in private universities, 15 per cent in public universities, 14 per cent in public liberal arts colleges, and 2 per cent in technological institutions. However, there are differences based upon the type of institution the president now heads. For example, a large percentage of the presidents of public colleges and universities received their bachelor's degrees in public institutions, while a majority of the presidents of private institutions received their undergraduate degrees at privately-supported institutions.

About 44 per cent of the public university presidents received their undergraduate degrees in public universities and 45 per cent of public liberal arts presidents received their degrees in public col-

TABLE 23
TYPES OF INSTITUTIONS GRANTING DEGREES TO PRESIDENTS

	Percentage of Presidents									
	University				Liberal Arts					All
Type of Institution	Pub.	Cath.	Prot.	Indep.	Pub.	Cath.	Prot.	Indep.	Tech.	Pres.
A. Bachelor's Degree										
Private college	36	6	53	62	25	67	73	65	12	52
Private university	10	87	39	19	11	25	13	16	19	17
Public college	10	0	5	4	45	4	4	4	19	14
Public university	44	0	5	15	18	3	9	12	19	15
Technological institution	0	6	0	0	1	1	1	3	31	2
Total per cent	100	100*	100*	100	100	100	100	100	100	100
B. Master's Degree										
Private college	11	8	20	36	4	8	14	23	6	12
Private university	26	92	53	41	33	85	41	38	27	45
Public college	6	0	0	5	11	0	7	5	6	6
Public university	57	0	27	18	52	7	38	34	40	36
Technological institution	0	0	0	0	0	0	0	0	21	1
Total per cent	100	100	100	100	100	100	100	100	100	100
C. Doctor's Degree										
Private university	37	67	69	86	43	91	54	70	55	60
Public university	63	33	31	14	57	9	46	30	45	40
Total per cent	100	100	100	100	100	100	100	100	100	100

*Does not total 100 per cent exactly due to rounding of figures.

leges. Among Catholic institution presidents, about 92 per cent received their degrees in private institutions with nearly all the university presidents educated in Catholic universities, and over two-thirds the Catholic college presidents educated in Catholic liberal arts colleges. The presidents of Protestant-related and independent institutions were educated primarily in private institutions. Almost one-third of the presidents of technological institutions received their undergraduate degrees in technological or military academies and institutions, while a relatively similar percentage were educated in the other types of public and private universities.

Colleges and universities where the academic presidents took their undergraduate programs represent different types of institutions throughout the country. The data revealed that 19 per cent of the presidents in this study received their undergraduate education in the East North Central states, 17 per cent in the West North Central states, 15 per cent in the Middle Atlantic states, 12 per cent in the South Atlantic states, 11 per cent in Washington, D.C., and 10 per cent in New England.

At the master's level there was, as might be expected, movement away from the important sources of undergraduate education, that is, the liberal arts colleges, to the centers of graduate programs, the universities. Table 23 data show the types of institutions where the 590 academic presidents who earned master's degrees completed that level.

The academic presidents are seen attending private and public universities in much larger percentages. The largest percentage still attended private institutions, mainly the private universities, but a growing percentage also turned to public universities. The public liberal arts colleges were attended for master's degrees in education. The presidents of public institutions attended public universities in much greater percentages than did the presidents of private institutions, and the presidents of private institutions were more likely to have attended private universities.

When comparisons were made of the regions where presidents received their master's degrees and their bachelor's degrees, there were increased percentages for master's work in the colleges and universities in the New England, Middle Atlantic, Washington, D.C., and the East North Central regions. Types of universities most frequently attended included private universities in the New England and Middle Atlantic regions, and state universities in the

East North Central regions. There were reduced percentages of presidents earning master's degrees in the South Atlantic, East South Central, West South Central, and West North Central states. Approximately the same percentages earned master's degrees as those who earned bachelor's degrees in the Mountain and Pacific regions.

The academic presidents earned their doctoral degrees at both private and public universities. Following the pattern observed at the undergraduate and master's levels, the presidents of public institutions were more likely to have been educated at the doctoral level in public rather than private universities. On the whole, about 60 per cent of all academic presidents received their doctoral training in private universities. It is interesting to note that one-third of the Catholic university presidents earned doctorates in public universities, while none of these men were educated in public institutions prior to the doctoral level. However, over 90 per cent of the presidents of Catholic liberal arts colleges earned doctoral degrees at private, Catholic institutions.

An analysis of the regions where these doctoral-level institutions are located shows that about 60 per cent are found in three regions: East North Central (25 per cent), Middle Atlantic (22 per cent), and New England (13 per cent). In the East North Central states, the universities most often attended were the state universities and a few private universities; in the Middle Atlantic states, nearly all attended private universities; and in New England, nearly all attended private universities. About 10 per cent of all presidents received doctorates in the West North Central states (mainly at state universities); 7 per cent received doctorates in the Pacific region in similar proportions at public and private universities; and 6 per cent earned their doctorates in private universities in the nation's capital.

The significance of the doctorate for entry into—as well as mobility within—higher education has led to an examination to determine if certain universities were attended more frequently than others at that level of formal training. It is important to point out that the actual choice of an institution by each person is a complex and often subtle process and is related to a great number of factors. A number of interrelated issues were pursued: whether certain institutions seemed to be perceived as the most desirable choices (for whatever reasons) among the presidents; whether a relatively small number of universities were responsible for the professional training of these individuals; and whether the presidents earned their doctorates randomly in universities throughout the nation.

The names of universities granting doctorates to at least ten academic presidents in the sample are listed in Table 24, where it can be seen that about 57 per cent of the presidents received their doctorates in one of sixteen universities. Moreover, four private universities granted doctorates to 22 per cent of the presidents: Chicago, Columbia, Harvard, and Catholic University. Of these sixteen universities, five are in the Ivy League: Columbia, Harvard, Yale, Cornell, and Pennsylvania; five are large state universities in the Midwest: Iowa, Ohio State, Wisconsin, Michigan, and Illinois; three are Catholic universities: Catholic University in Washington, D.C., Fordham University, and St. Louis University; two are private universities: Chicago and New York University; and one is is a public university in the West, University of California at Berkeley.

An analysis of institutions attended for doctoral training reveals that the presidents of public institutions mainly attended Midwestern state universities, along with a concentration in four private universities (Harvard, Columbia, Chicago, and New York Univer-

TABLE 24
UNIVERSITIES GRANTING THE MOST DOCTORATES TO ACADEMIC PRESIDENTS

Name of University	Number of Presidents	Cumulative Percentage*
University of Chicago	30	5.9
Columbia University	29	11.5
Harvard University	28	17.0
Catholic University	28	22.4
Yale University	19	26.1
University of Iowa	18	29.7
New York University	18	33.3
Ohio State University	18	36.8
University of Wisconsin	18	40.3
University of Michigan	16	43.4
Fordham University	15	46.3
Cornell University	14	49.2
St. Louis University	12	51.5
University of Illinois	11	53.6
University of Pennsylvania	11	55.7
University of California (Berkeley)	10	57.6

*The percentages were based upon the 512 individuals who gave a specific name of university where the doctorate was earned.

sity). A majority of those attending Columbia were graduates of Columbia's Teachers College. The presidents of Catholic institutions attended Catholic universities (Catholic University, Fordham, St. Louis, and Notre Dame), and they also attended universities outside the United States (Rome and Toronto). The presidents of private, non-Catholic institutions were most likely to have attended Harvard, Yale, Columbia, or Chicago.

In short, while the presidents of colleges and universities attended a great variety of institutions at each degree level, a relatively small number of universities were attended by the presidents at the doctoral level.

Relatively few academic presidents earned academic degrees at foreign universities. A few had studied abroad for a short period of time, but most academic presidents have not pursued formal studies outside the United States. For the small number who did study abroad, the most often-mentioned institutions were Oxford, Cambridge, Rome, and Toronto.

There is some suggestion in the more popular literature that a number of college and university presidents were at one time students at their present institutions. It has been implied that alumni of institutions are often considered and finally selected by boards of trustees who attempt to fill vacancies in the presidential office. This idea was tested using questionnaire responses, and a summary is presented in Table 25. About 23 per cent of all academic presidents

TABLE 25
PRESIDENTS EARNING A DEGREE AT THEIR PRESENT INSTITUTION

Presidents' Institutions	Did Not Earn a Degree (per cent)	Did Earn a Degree (per cent)
Public university	87	13
Catholic university	55	45
Protestant-related university	81	19
Independent university	93	7
Public liberal arts	87	13
Catholic liberal arts	55	45
Protestant-related liberal arts	77	23
Independent liberal arts	83	17
Technological	92	8
Total per cent for all presidents	77	23

NOTE: This does not include honorary degrees awarded by institutions but only academic degrees granted by virtue of completing a formal undergraduate or graduate program.

in the study earned an undergraduate or graduate degree at the institution they now head, but there are some variations. For example, about 45 per cent of the presidents of Catholic institutions received degrees (nearly all, undergraduate) at their present institutions. It can be seen that a relatively larger percentage of private, non-Catholic liberal arts presidents are alumni of their present institutions than is the case for their counterparts in the private universities. There is evidence that, in general, about two out of ten academic presidents are alumni of their present institutions. The ratio more than doubles for presidents of Catholic institutions, is somewhat less for the presidents of public institutions, and is about equal for the presidents of private, non-Catholic institutions.

Special mention has been made that aspects of the social origins of the presidents seemed to be similar among those individuals now in similar types of institutions. It is clear that the formal, educational training received by presidents associated with each major type of institution—public, Catholic, Protestant-related, or independent—is also quite similar. Differences become more noticeable when careers of presidents of different types of institutions are contrasted. There is strong reason to believe that experiences, models, values, and philosophies were largely formulated in and associated with the kind of institution the president now heads, as well as those values associated with social and family origins. This theme carries through into the presidents' full time careers.

7

Career Patterns

Although career changes are often due to external factors in a person's environment, important changes quite often are found within the upwardly mobile person himself. Some modern writers have discussed the internal factors by referring to personality attributes and psychological drives. Approaches are also found which describe an individual's career pattern as an on-going discovery of who he is or who he would like to be, an unconscious and continual development into a more fully functioning human being, or a greater capacity to persist, to act, to achieve power, and so on. The inner psychological drives and individual variations in the academic president's career were not the subject for this research, but it was possible to obtain a perspective on the major career patterns formed throughout the person's full-time career. In a study that closely followed the president's career at regular intervals from the time he first began working full time to his present position, these questions were considered: What sequence of occupations did the presidents hold prior to assuming the presidency? How long did it take to move from the first full-time positions to the presidency? At what age did the individuals assume the presidency and how long have they been in the positions? What have been the educational experiences either as teachers or administrators prior to becoming presidents? What were the immediate springboards to the presidency? How many of these individuals have established their careers at more than one institution? How many have been presidents of other institutions as well as the institution each now heads?

The careers of the great majority of academic presidents in this study began and continued in education and professional fields. Two-thirds of these presidents began their careers in education while one-third of them started out as elementary or secondary school teachers. About 26 per cent began as teachers at the college level. It was interesting, and somewhat surprising to find that only 3 per cent of the presidents began their careers in educational administration at the college level. When other professions were examined, it was found that about 17 per cent began their careers in religious service with another 6 per cent in the medical, legal, engineering, and other recognized professions. Contrary to popular belief, relatively few academic presidents began or spent significant parts of their careers in business (5 per cent), government (2 per cent), military (3 per cent), or farming (0.3 per cent) occupations.

Over the twenty years of their careers as shown in Table 26 there was a continuously growing percentage of presidents in education, while the number of those in other major occupational categories steadily decreased. Five years after their careers began, many of the presidents left teaching at the elementary or secondary level, while there were increases in principal or superintendent positions, college faculty, and administrative positions in higher education.

The category of other professions declined from 23 to 13 per cent and many of those in religious service turned to education.[1] At the end of five years, there were decreases in business and government, and a slight rise in military service where many of the men fulfilled regular military obligations.

Ten years later the basic trends continued with 84 per cent engaged in education and 10 per cent in other professions. Within the education category, there was a further movement away from teaching at the elementary-secondary levels. In addition, there was

1. The category of "clergy and religious" includes the heads of Catholic institutions—priests and sisters—and some Protestant clergymen who began their careers in religious service and were called upon to serve the church in its higher educational program.

TABLE 26
CAREER SEQUENCE FOR ACADEMIC PRESIDENTS

President's Occupation	Beginning Occupation (per cent)	5 Years Later (per cent)	10 Years Later (per cent)	15 Years Later (per cent)	20 Years Later (per cent)
Education	67	77	84	88	92
Elementary-secondary teacher	33	13	5	1	0*
Principal, superintendent	2	12	8	6	3
College faculty	26	32	26	14	5
Chairman of department	1	7	11	7	5
Dean of college	1	4	9	11	7
College administrator: below vice-president	3	4	8	8	3
College administrator: vice-president	0*	3	6	11	6
College president	1	2	11	30	63
Other Professions	23	13	10	7	4
Clergy or religious	17	8	6	4	2
Other professions	6	5	4	3	2
Business	5	3	1	1	1
Laborer	1	0	0	0	0
White-collar	2	1	0	0	0
Minor executive	1	1	0*	0*	0*
Major executive	1	1	1	1	1
Business owner	0*	0*	0*	0*	0*
Other	5	6	4	4	2
Government	2	1	2	2	1
Military	3	5	2	2	1
Farmer	0*	0	0	0	0
Total per cent	100	100	100	100	100

*Less than 0.5 per cent. Total number: 760.

a beginning movement out of principal, superintendent, and college faculty statuses. Many presidents moved into positions as department chairmen, college deans, lower level administrators, and academic vice-presidents. After ten years in their careers, 11 per cent of these people were selected to a college presidency.

At the end of fifteen years, 88 per cent of the presidents were in education and 7 per cent were in the other professions. Only 5 per cent continued their careers in business, government, or military service. Again if we look closely at the education category, only 1 per cent of the individuals were school teachers, 6 per cent were principals or superintendents, and 14 per cent were college teachers. A fairly high percentage had moved to higher administrative levels in colleges as 11 per cent were vice-presidents and 30 per cent were college presidents.

Twenty years after their careers began, 92 per cent of the presidents were in education and only 3 per cent were in business, government, and military service. An analysis of the education category reveals that about 63 per cent had attained the presidency.

Thus, the career lines of academic presidents clearly run through educational and professional categories; no more than 10 per cent spent an appreciable number of years in either business, government, or military service. These individuals made their way in the professions and used the educational arena as the means of upward or lateral occupational mobility rather than business or government.

Public Universities

About two-thirds of the presidents of public universities began their careers as teachers at the elementary-secondary levels (20 per cent) and college level (43 per cent). After five years, only 3 per cent remained as elementary-secondary schoolteachers, and 10 per cent became principals or superintendents. At the same time, many presidents had already moved into academic administration positions as departmental chairmen (8 per cent), college deans (6 per cent), and college administrators (9 per cent).

At the end of ten years, there was a movement to higher level academic administrative positions in colleges: 16 per cent were department chairmen, 10 per cent were college deans, and 9 per cent were academic vice-presidents. At the end of ten years, one-half the public university presidents were in academic administration at the college level.

At the fifteen-year career mark, only 1 per cent remained in elementary-secondary education and 13 per cent were college teachers. The largest increases were at the college deanship level (22 per cent) and the academic vice-presidency (20 per cent). Finally, at the end of twenty years, 61 per cent were academic presidents, with another 20 per cent at the dean and vice-president levels. The greatest increase into the academic president group occurred between fifteen and twenty years in their careers. And, for a still large percentage (39 per cent), selection to a college presidency occurred after a career of already twenty years, mainly in higher education.

Catholic Universities

It must be recalled that the presidents of Catholic institutions in this study are all priests or nuns of the Roman Catholic faith. Thus, to speak about career patterns for these men and women one cannot overlook the fact that if a so-called career choice were made it was essentially to the church and to a particular religious order. For a number of these individuals, their career patterns should be explained largely as priests or nuns who assumed particular responsibilities in the church over an extended period of time. But for purposes here, only their movement through positions in Catholic education will be noted, while holding in view the fact that their careers were intertwined with long training, aspirations, and preparation as priests or nuns.

Five years after completing preparation for the priesthood, most Catholic university presidents were faculty members (25 per cent), college deans (30 per cent), and department chairmen (10 per cent), while one man was a president. Ten years later, all priests were in high academic administrative positions and 35 per cent were university presidents. Fifteen years later, 75 per cent of the men had been selected to the presidency and another 15 per cent were vice-presidents. At twenty years later, 80 per cent of the men were university presidents. Once becoming a priest, these people moved fairly quickly to high levels of administrative responsibility in Catholic universities.

Private (Non-Catholic) Universities

Because of the great similarities in basic career patterns of the Protestant-related and independent university presidents, they will be discussed together. At the beginning of their careers, 88 per cent were in education, including 44 per cent as college faculty members and 14 per cent as elementary-secondary teachers. Another 14 per cent began their careers as Protestant clergymen. Five years later, there was the customary movement from teaching at the elementary-secondary levels to positions as principals and super-intendents. In addition, there was movement into college faculty and academic administrative positions. Ten years later the trend into higher level academic administrative positions continued with a number leaving strictly faculty positions and becoming department chairmen (10 per cent), college deans (14 per cent), and college administrators (14 per cent).

Fifteen years later marked the first major movement into the college presidency (26 per cent), the college vice-presidency (20 per cent) and dean or department head (20 per cent). At the twenty year point in the career of these men, 51 per cent had attained the presidency and 11 per cent were vice-presidents. This, of course, also meant that almost half the men would attain the presidency after a career of at least twenty years, spent primarily in higher education. The presidents of private, non-Catholic universities spent relatively longer periods of time in levels directly beneath the president, such as dean or vice-president, than is true for the presidents of other institutions.

Public Liberal Arts Colleges

About 60 per cent of the public liberal arts presidents began their careers as teachers in elementary-secondary schools (a percentage equalled only by the presidents of Catholic liberal arts colleges). Only 20 per cent actually began their careers as college faculty members or college administrators. Five years later, however, the percentage in elementary-secondary teaching dropped sharply to 14 per cent. A majority of these people moved quickly into a position as principal or superintendent, evidenced by the fact that 30 per cent were in the latter positions by five years. Also, a number of public liberal arts presidents turned to college teaching, as the percentage nearly doubled to 30 per cent.

Ten years later, greater movement into college administration occurred and only 5 per cent remained as elementary-secondary teachers. The number who were principals or superintendents also fell, while 12 per cent became department chairmen; 7 per cent, college deans; and 10 per cent, college administrators. Fifteen years later, almost one-fourth were college presidents and only 13 per cent remained in elementary or secondary schools.

After a career of twenty years, six out of ten had been selected to a college presidency with another 6 per cent as vice-presidents and 10 per cent college deans. Out of all public liberal arts presidents, only 1 per cent were still engaged in a career outside education.

Catholic Liberal Arts Colleges

The point made for Catholic university presidents regarding their intertwined careers in religious service and Catholic higher education applies generally to Catholic liberal arts presidents as well. After acceptance as a priest or nun, 61 per cent became elementary-secondary teachers while another 24 per cent moved into college teaching. Five years later, only 38 per cent were still elementary-secondary teachers while the percentage in college teaching and administration rose.

After ten years, only 23 per cent were in elementary-secondary education, with the remainder in higher education. After fifteen years, about one-third were chosen for the presidency and another third were either department chairmen, college deans, or college administrators. After twenty years, more than two-thirds were presidents, replicating the pattern of Catholic university presidents, that is, once becoming a priest or nun, there was rapid movement to high levels of responsibility. However, while Catholic university presidents did not hold positions in elementary-secondary education and remained in universities, the majority of Catholic liberal arts presidents began in elementary-secondary schools. Much of this can be explained by the work of particular religious orders, and by the fact that the church depended heavily upon the sisters and their teaching orders to work with the extensive education program at the lower levels.

Private Liberal Arts Colleges

The presidents of private, Protestant-related and independent liberal arts colleges show quite similar career lines and are again discussed as one group. Three major categories account for three-fourths of the first positions held by private liberal arts presidents: college faculty (27 per cent), elementary-secondary teaching (25 per cent), and Protestant clergy (24 per cent). Five years later, the typical movement from elementary-secondary teaching into positions as principal or superintendent, college teaching, and academic administration in higher education occurred. At the ten year point, the movement accelerated into higher levels of academic administration: college deans (7 per cent), college administration (9 per cent), academic vice-presidents (6 per cent), and college presidents (12 per cent).

Fifteen years later, more than one-third were college presidents and 8 per cent were vice-presidents. After a career of twenty years, the percentage selected to the presidency nearly doubled to 69 per cent, with another 12 per cent either academic vice-presidents or college deans.

Technological Institutions

The presidents of technological institutions (including four military college presidents) began their careers in three major occupational categories: elementary-secondary education (31 per cent), college faculty (31 per cent), and as engineers in business and industry (22 per cent). After five years, the movement out of elementary-secondary teaching took place with corresponding increases in principal or superintendent positions, college faculty, and department chairman statuses. At ten years, none of the men remained in elementary-secondary teaching or administration, while more rose to higher levels of educational administration.

After fifteen years, still greater percentages moved into higher levels, although only 17 per cent were actually selected to the presidency. After twenty years, 35 per cent were presidents, and 22 per cent were vice-presidents and deans. Among all types of academic presidents, the heads of technological institutions remained in careers—usually in education, business, and the military—for extended periods before being selected for a college presidency. The fact that only 35 per cent had attained the presidency after a career of twenty years means that almost two-thirds were selected to the position after a fairly extensive career in other areas. This 35 per cent represented almost half that for the other presidents at similar stages in their careers. Many of the presidents of military colleges were in strictly military settings for substantial portions of their careers prior to being chosen to head military colleges.

Female Academic Presidents

The career patterns of women academic presidents have not yet been examined separately, but have been included among the liberal arts presidents' career lines. It should be recalled that 87 per cent of the 84 female presidents (or 73 women) were heads of Catholic liberal arts colleges, thus their career lines were included in the discussion of presidents of Catholic liberal arts colleges.

The career lines of women are very similar to the basic patterns of all academic presidents. However, a much higher percentage of women (nearly two-thirds) began their careers as elementary-secondary teachers and another 17 per cent began in college teaching, as shown in Table 27. Over the fifteen years there was general movement from elementary-secondary teaching into college teaching and administration. After fifteen years, only 18 per cent were presidents, but during the interval from fifteen to twenty years, there was a sharp increase to 64 per cent for those reaching the

TABLE 27
CAREER SEQUENCE FOR FEMALE ACADEMIC PRESIDENTS

Occupation	First Position (per cent)	5 Years Later (per cent)	10 Years Later (per cent)	15 Years Later (per cent)	20 Years Later (per cent)
Elementary-secondary teacher	63	49	23	7	1
Principal, superintendent	1	5	7	6	6
College faculty	17	25	38	21	8
Department chairman	0	4	12	12	9
College dean	0	4	6	10	6
College Administrator: below vice-president	0	3	5	12	4
College administrator: vice-president	0	0	2	10	2
College president	0	0	5	18	64
Other education	0	4	0	4	0
Other professions	9	3	0	0	0
Business	8	3	2	0	0
Government	2	0	0	0	0
Total per cent	100	100	100	100	100
Total number: 84					

presidency. The women seemed to spend a somewhat longer period of time in positions throughout the educational hierarchy relative to the men, but for women and men, the major move to the presidency came between fifteen and twenty years in the career. Few women spent significant portions of their full-time careers outside education.

Tenure in Office

Along with a study of the general occupational steps followed by academic presidents over a twenty-year period beginning with their first full-time positions, another career-related framework is interesting. It was pointed out earlier that a relatively large percentage of presidents had not been selected to the presidency during or up to twenty years of full-time work and that a number were chosen after that time. For many who completed all their education and then began working full-time, this would place their age at about twenty-five to twenty-seven and it suggests that many did not attain the presidency until their late forties or older. Others took an undergraduate or graduate degree, interrupted their education by a full-time job for a few years or by military service, and then went back to college to finish their advanced degrees. For this latter group, setting a meaningful beginning date to their careers is much more difficult. However, it would be well for us to have a context of time that complements the discussion of occupational sequence and thus increases our understanding of how long it took to achieve the presidency.

With this in mind, our research examines: (1) how old the presidents were when they assumed their present positions, and (2) how long the presidents have been in their present positions.

On the average, college and university presidents in this study assumed their present positions at about forty-five years of age. The presidents of public universities, independent universities, and technological institutions were somewhat older on the average, but most were around forty-five. When an analysis was made based upon tenure in office, no noticeable differences were observed. The average age of those presidents selected during 1967–68 was 45.6 years and that figure held for presidents who had been in office for longer periods of time. The only serious deviation took place with those presidents who had been in office longer than twenty years. In this latter case, their average age upon assuming the presidency was only 37.8. There were no differences in starting ages when presidents of institutions in various regions were compared or when men and women were compared.

A summary is given in Table 28 showing the ages of the presidents in 1968. Based upon these data the average age of academic presidents is 52.9 years, with a range in ages from twenty-nine to seventy years. As a subgroup, the presidents of Catholic institutions tend to be younger than the presidents of other institutions, reflecting, as pointed out earlier, that the presidents of Catholic in-

TABLE 28
AGES OF ACADEMIC PRESIDENTS

Presidents' Institutions	Average (mean) Age in 1968	Range in Ages (years)
Public university	54.1	39 to 67
Catholic university	50.7	40 to 63
Protestant-related university	57.5	45 to 68
Independent university	53.4	41 to 64
Public liberal arts	53.5	32 to 69
Catholic liberal arts	51.0	32 to 68
Protestant-related liberal arts	52.4	29 to 70
Independent liberal arts	53.2	35 to 69
Technological	54.6	42 to 66
Present age for all presidents:	52.9	29 to 70

stitutions moved up faster to the presidency relative to the others (after fifteen years in their careers, a majority had already reached the presidency). The other subgroups of presidents tend to cluster around the fifty-three years mark, with the exception of Protestant-related university presidents who average around fifty-seven years of age. In addition, the presidents of the universities tend to be generally a little older than the presidents of the liberal arts colleges.

It was found that those presidents who have been in office for longer periods of time are progressively older than those recently chosen for the presidency. The following breakdown shows the average age based on tenure in office:

Presidents who were chosen:	*Average present age:*
within 1967–68	46.4
within 1962–67	48.9
within 1957–62	53.7
within 1952–57	57.4
within 1947–52	59.6
during 1947	62.4

The average college or university president has been in his present position for 7.8 years, although there are differences among presidents of various types of institutions. For example, the average Protestant-related university president has been in office for nearly twelve years, while the average public university president has been in office for only about seven years, according to data in Table 29.

TABLE 29
YEARS IN PRESENT POSITION

Presidents' Institutions	Average Years in Position
Public university	6.9
Catholic university	5.7
Protestant-related university	11.8
Independent university	5.6
Public liberal arts	8.2
Catholic liberal arts	6.6
Protestant-related liberal arts	8.2
Independent liberal arts	9.6
Technological	8.0
Average number of years for all presidents:	7.8

An analysis was also made of the number of years in the present position by region of the country to see if there was more movement in and out of the presidency in some areas and not others (Table 30). The region of the country where the institution is located did not seem to be associated with differences in the number of years the president has held his present position. In most cases, the average tenures still cluster around 7.8 years. College presidents in the Pacific and West South Central states have held their positions somewhat longer, while the presidents of institutions in the Mountain and New England states have somewhat shorter tenures in office. Tenure related to the size of the institution presents no new patterns

TABLE 30
YEARS IN PRESENT POSITION, BY REGION

Presidents' Institutions by Census Regions	Average Years in Position
New England	7.1
Middle Atlantic	7.3
South Atlantic	7.9
East South Central	7.6
West South Central	8.2
East North Central	7.7
West North Central	7.0
Mountain	6.6
Pacific	8.7

with the single exception of the largest universities (over 30,000 students). In this case, the average tenure in the present position is 9.5 years or higher than the average of 7.8 years. Once under the 30,000 student enrollment, no deviations of more than 0.5 per cent are found.

Some Crucial Avenues to the Presidency

Consideration of the sequence of occupations and the number of years spent on the way to and in the presidency now lead to an examination of two crucial avenues in the presidents' career mobility. First, it is well-recognized that about 90 per cent of the academic presidents spent their lives in educational and major professional endeavors, and that a large number were college faculty members at various points in their careers. Since those with faculty experiences are a fairly distinguishable group and since some writers state that the ideal academic president is one with faculty experience, an analysis is presented of these men as professors en route to the presidency. What academic ranks did they attain before attaining the presidency? With which academic departments were they associated? How many years did they serve as faculty members? It is recalled that a study of how many of the presidents were students at the institutions they now head was conducted, and this prompted an inquiry into how many were teachers at the institution they now head.

Second, it is obvious that some presidents did not use the avenue of college teaching to the presidency, but were in college administration or occupations outside higher education. Some writers have suggested that the position held before becoming president is the best indicator of where presidents are sought by boards of trustees and where the most valuable training for a presidency takes place. Thus, we now take a close look at the last positions held by academic presidents prior to assuming the presidency. Some of the questions to be answered include: How many men came directly from another college presidency? a college deanship? a foundation office? a government position? a business position? The analysis will also reveal the number of individuals that moved up to the presidency from within versus without the institution they now head.

Prior Experiences
as Faculty Members

It is occasionally said that many academic presidents have never spent time in the college classroom as teaching or research faculty members, although it is never made clear what percentage "many" is supposed to represent. Table 31 summarizes the percentages of presidents with and without college teaching experience. About 86 per cent of all presidents have had some college teaching experience, with the percentage varying slightly by presidents' types of institu-

TABLE 31
COLLEGE LEVEL TEACHING EXPERIENCE

Presidents' Institutions	Percentage With Teaching Experience	Percentage Without Teaching Experience
Public university	94	6
Catholic university	85	15
Protestant-related university	76	24
Independent university	93	7
Public liberal arts	89	11
Catholic liberal arts	92	8
Protestant-related liberal arts	72	28
Independent liberal arts	93	7
Technological	75	25
All presidents	86	14

tions. For the presidents of Protestant-related universities and colleges and technological institutions, the percentage who have had college teaching experience drops to about 75 per cent. In the case of Protestant-related institution presidents, a relatively larger percentage were ministers for the major parts of their careers and most moved directly into academic administration. In the case of technological institution presidents, a relatively larger percentage moved into a level of academic administration directly from business without any actual college teaching experience.

Thus, it is clear that more than eight out of ten presidents have had college teaching experience. College teaching experience is still a fairly general category, however, and there are well-recognized levels or ranks within the college teaching profession that to a large extent reflect the duration, commitment, and capability as a college teacher. The ranks in descending order in the academic hierarchy are: professor, associate professor, assistant professor, instructor, and lecturer. The full professor stands at the top of the profession in terms of recognition from his colleagues. As a senior faculty member he has had at least seven or eight years of teaching experience and his promotions have usually been tied to demonstrated competence in his field. The assistant professorial rank is regarded as the starting place for full-time college teachers although the instructor level also has that place. The rank of lecturer is a complex one in that it may be a part-time position and commitment to college teaching per se, and in some cases a lecturer of some distinction receives a higher financial compensation than a professor. It is not for us to discuss the complexities and often subtleties that are a part of faculty promotion, but simply to recognize these basic patterns of rank that are unique to the academic community. The question becomes: what was the highest rank attained by these individuals as faculty members prior to being selected to the presidency?[2]

The percentage of presidents with teaching experience is shown in Table 31, while Table 32 gives the highest rank attained by those

2. The faculty rank prior to becoming president was used because it represents a more accurate reflection of one's recognition by peers as a faculty member. In most cases, the academic presidency carries with it the rank of professor, and if a new president had not attained that rank through the more conventional process in an academic department, he would then receive it along with the position of presidency. Thus, nearly all presidents have a rank of professor, but to make matters clear, only those attaining the rank as a faculty member not as an academic administrator are included.

TABLE 32
HIGHEST FACULTY RANK PRIOR TO PRESIDENCY

Presidents' Institutions	Lecturer (per cent)	Instructor (per cent)	Assistant Professor (per cent)	Associate Professor (per cent)	Professor (per cent)
Public university	4	4	4	8	80
Catholic university	6	0	47	6	41
Protestant university	0	6	19	6	69
Independent university	8	4	0	4	84
Public liberal arts	7	9	9	14	61
Catholic liberal arts	4	19	23	13	41
Protestant liberal arts	8	9	11	13	59
Independent liberal arts	6	11	15	14	54
Technological	8	4	12	8	68
Per cent for all presidents	6	9	13	12	60

presidents who had college teaching experience prior to being selected for the presidency. Of the academic presidents with college teaching experience, 60 per cent had attained the highest rank of professor prior to being chosen for the presidency, 12 per cent had attained the rank of associate professor, 13 per cent had attained the rank of assistant professor, and 15 per cent had been either instructors or lecturers. Over 80 per cent of the presidents of public universities and independent universities were full professors, while only about 41 per cent of the presidents of Catholic institutions had a full professor rank. In the Catholic institutions, 47 per cent in the uni-

TABLE 33
COLLEGE LEVEL TEACHING BACKGROUND

Presidents' Institutions	Number of Years College-Level Teaching Experience				
	1–5 (per cent)	6–10 (per cent)	11–15 (per cent)	16–20 (per cent)	Over 20 (per cent)
Public university	19	20	27	18	16
Catholic university	38	25	31	6	0
Protestant university	20	26	40	7	7
Independent university	19	29	38	5	9
Public liberal arts	30	19	27	15	9
Catholic liberal arts	32	30	27	5	6
Protestant liberal arts	25	24	29	13	9
Independent liberal arts	21	21	37	15	6
Technological	22	17	44	17	0
Per cent for all presidents	26	23	30	13	8

versities attained only the rank of assistant professor and instructor, and 42 per cent in the colleges attained no higher than those ranks. Data concerning the total number of years that these same individuals were college faculty members prior to becoming academic presidents are listed in Table 33, with the number of years of teaching experience broken down into five-year intervals.

About one-fourth of all the presidents in this study had up to five years teaching experience and about one-half had been college teachers for ten years or less. Thirty per cent had between eleven and fifteen years teaching experience and 21 per cent had more than fifteen years teaching experience at the college level. It is interesting to note that the presidents of Catholic institutions had relatively fewer years experience in college teaching than the other presidents. Another figure that stands out is the 34 per cent of the public university presidents with over fifteen years teaching experience (16 per cent of whom had taught for over twenty years).

Thus, academic presidents have varying tenure as faculty members, although the average is close to 10.5 years for all presidents. It is somewhat less for the presidents of Catholic institutions and somewhat higher for presidents of public universities, private non-Catholic universities, private independent liberal arts colleges, and technological institutions.

Another matter of interest related to the presidents' faculty experiences is the kind of academic departments with which they were affiliated. In most cases, there is an obvious and direct relationship between the academic department and the formal education of the presidents (especially at the doctoral level), but occasionally some taught in other areas of interest. A tabulation of departments grouped by major fields is given in Table 34 for those with college teaching experience, showing that the disciplines in the humanities, education, social sciences, and natural sciences were the major fields of 82 per cent of the academic presidents.

Twelve leading departmental disciplines within the major fields of study are listed in Table 35; 71 per cent of the presidents in this study who were college-level teachers were affiliated with these twelve departments. No significant patterns are observed in comparing presidents of different types of institutions. However, almost 20 per cent of the individuals who head public colleges and universities taught educational administration. English and history as teaching areas are well represented across all types of institutions. Religion or

TABLE 34

ACADEMIC DEPARTMENT AFFILIATIONS WHILE FACULTY MEMBERS

Departments Grouped by Major Fields	Percentage of University Presidents				Percentage of Liberal Arts Presidents					Percentage of All
	Public	Cath.	Prot.	Indep.	Public	Cath.	Prot.	Indep.	Techn.	Presidents
Agricultural	5	0	0	0	4	0	1	0	0	2
Business	9	0	11	23	7	6	8	11	13	8
Engineering	1	0	0	4	2	3	0	0	50	3
Natural Science	14	18	24	11	9	19	9	9	21	12
Medical-Legal	7	0	6	0	0	0	1	3	0	2
Education	18	12	6	11	43	9	8	6	8	17
Communications	4	0	0	0	3	0	8	0	4	3
Humanities	25	65	53	39	19	50	47	53	4	38
Social Science	17	5	0	12	13	13	18	18	0	15
Total per cent	100	100	100	100	100	100	100	100	100	100

TABLE 35

LEADING ACADEMIC DEPARTMENTS

Department	Percentage of Presidents
Humanities:	
English	11
History	10
Religion, Theology	8
Philosophy	5
Natural Sciences:	
Chemistry	4
Business:	
Economics*	5
Education:	
Educational administration	11
Guidance	3
Social Sciences:	
Sociology	4
Political Science	4
Psychology	3
Communications:	
Speech	3
Total per cent	71

*Many colleges and universities place the economics department within the social science area rather than business.

theology departments are especially found among Protestant liberal arts college presidents. More than 40 per cent of the Catholic liberal arts presidents taught in four departments: English, 15 per cent; theology, 10 per cent; philosophy, 9 per cent; and chemistry, 9 per cent. The presidents of technological institutions are heavily represented in all engineering departments. In another analysis investigating the types of institutions at which these persons taught, the data showed that these individuals taught at a variety of institutions throughout the country at each rank. Brief sketches of the patterns for each grouping of presidents follow.

Presidents of public universities. The great majority of public university presidents who were college teachers taught in public universities and colleges. At the instructor level, slightly over one-half taught in public higher education and at each successively higher rank there was a clear move to public higher education. As assistant professors, 70 per cent taught in public universities; as associate professors, nearly 80 per cent were so associated; and as full professors, slightly over 80 per cent taught in public universities, with another 15 per cent teaching in public colleges. Although they taught in all regions of the nation, most of the full professors taught in the state universities in the East North Central states, led by Michigan State University (four persons), University of Illinois (four persons), University of Michigan (three men), and the state universities of Kentucky (three men), and California at Los Angeles (three men).

Presidents of Catholic universities. All the Catholic university presidents in the sample who were college teachers taught in Catholic institutions, mainly universities. Two men taught at the University of Detroit while other universities represented were Bradley, St. Louis, Creighton, Niagara, Villanova, and Boston College.

Presidents of Protestant-related and independent universities. The presidents of private universities (non-Catholic) taught primarily in a variety of private colleges and universities at each rank. There were, however, more who taught at the Ivy League institutions of Harvard, Princeton, and Brown.

Presidents of public liberal arts colleges. Almost nine out of ten presidents did their college teaching in public colleges and universities. Institutions in all regions were well represented among the group—particularly the state colleges in the South Atlantic, West South Central, and West North Central states, and the state universities in the East North Central states. No specific institution had a concentration of more than two persons in this sample who taught at that institution, thus, as a group, the presidents of public liberal arts colleges are most representative of American public education.

Presidents of Catholic liberal arts colleges. As with the presidents of Catholic universities, the heads of the liberal arts colleges taught in Catholic institutions, with the vast majority teaching not in universities but rather in liberal arts colleges. No region stood out markedly from the others, although heavier concentrations were in the Middle Atlantic, East North Central, and West North Central states. Moreover, no one institution had more than two of these individuals as teachers.

Presidents of Protestant-related and independent liberal arts colleges. The presidents of these institutions had taught primarily in numerous private (non-Catholic) liberal arts colleges. The major regions where they taught included institutions in the East North Central, East South Central, South Atlantic, and Middle Atlantic states, but there was high dispersion among many private institutions.

Presidents of technological institutions. While the heads of the technological institutions taught mainly at technological institutions, many also taught in public and private universities and state colleges. These institutions were located mainly in the Middle Atlantic and East North Central states. Institutions represented included Massachusetts Institute of Technology, Brooklyn Polytechnic Institute, and the University of Rochester.

It is interesting that about 36 per cent of all academic presidents with college teaching experience taught at the institution they now head. This percentage applied to presidents of all types of institutions except for Catholic university and college presidents. In the latter cases, more than seven out of ten taught at the institutions they now head.

Although the presidents taught at a great many institutions throughout the country, a few patterns are predominant. Generally speaking, the presidents of public institutions who were former faculty members taught at public institutions, and the presidents of private institutions taught at private colleges and universities. Once again, the presidents' social origins, education, and aspects of their careers have been linked to associations with a given type of institution: public, Catholic, Protestant-related, independent, or technological. Such background experiences unquestionably helped influence the presidents' ultimate choices of the institutions they now head. The backgrounds of academic presidents when categorized by whether they served public, Catholic, Protestant-related, independent, or technological institutions become most revealing from the president's start in life to his present position.

Direct Springboard to Presidency

About one-third of all presidents in the sample moved to their position from inside the present institution while the remaining two-thirds came to the presidency from a position in another institution or organization.

Table 36 indicates the internal or external moves for the various types of presidents. Data show that it is much more likely that the

TABLE 36
How They Arrived at the Presidency

Presidents' Institutions	Internal Move (per cent)	External Move (per cent)
Public university	29	71
Catholic university	70	30
Protestant-related university	14	86
Independent university	29	71
Public liberal arts	22	78
Public liberal arts	71	29
Protestant liberal arts	19	81
Independent liberal arts	25	75
Technological	39	61
Average for all presidents	33	67

presidents of Catholic institutions held a prior position in their present institutions than as presidents of other institutions. Seven out of ten Catholic institution presidents made such an internal move. On the other hand, fewer than 20 per cent of the heads of Protestant-related colleges and universities were chosen from inside the institutions. In public institutions and independent institutions no more than three out of ten were selected from within, and in technological institutions almost four out of ten moved into the presidency from within the present institution.

When one examines the internal-external mobility issue over a period of time, no great deviations are noted. For example, of the sixty-one persons selected to the presidency during last year, 36 per cent were internal moves and 64 per cent were external. For the presidents selected during the last five years, 35 per cent were internal and 65 per cent were external. For those selected from five to ten years ago, 33 per cent were internal moves and 67 per cent represented external moves. For the presidents selected twenty years ago, 37 per cent were internal and 63 per cent were external moves. These data are not shown in the tables.

An analysis of the types of positions held by academic presidents immediately prior to assuming the presidency is given in Table 37. In general, the great majority of college and university presidents moved directly to the presidency from another position in education. Over three-fourths of the presidents came immediately from a higher education position, and at the upper levels, 22 per cent were college deans, 11 per cent were academic vice-presidents (or provosts), 11 per cent were department chairmen, and 10 per cent came from the faculty. Another 7 per cent were presidents of other colleges, 6 per cent were general administrative vice-presidents, 4 per cent were other college administrators, 3 per cent were deans of students, 2 per cent were assistants to presidents, 1 per cent were junior college presidents, and less than 1 per cent were serving as acting presidents. If the academic and administrative vice-presidents are combined into a general vice-president level, it can be seen that 17 per cent of the presidents came directly from that level.

Other educational positions were held by the academic presidents, including 3 per cent who were public school administrators, 1 per cent in state board of education positions, and 1 per cent who held offices in educational associations.

The next highest general occupational category that served as a springboard to the presidency was the Protestant clergy where 8 per cent or fifty-seven men moved directly from being a minister in a church to a college presidency.

About 3 per cent of the presidents came directly from government positions (primarily at the Federal level) and a little more than 1 per cent came from the military. It was somewhat surprising to find that contrary to speculation from some quarters, business directly supplied only about 2 per cent (or thirteen men) of the total aca-

TABLE 37

POSITIONS HELD BY ACADEMIC PRESIDENTS IMMEDIATELY PRIOR TO
ASSUMING THE PRESIDENCY

Prior Position Held	Percentage of University Presidents				Percentage of Liberal Arts Presidents					Percentage of All Presidents
	Public (n = 89)	Cath. (n = 19)	Prot. (n = 20)	Indep. (n = 28)	Public (n = 153)	Cath. (n = 129)	Prot. (n = 209)	Indep. (n = 72)	Techn. (n = 30)	(n = 750)
Education										
President of a college	19	5	15	18	6	0	6	7	4	7
Academic vice-pres. or provost	24	16	15	25	5	11	9	11	12	11
Administration, vice-president	7	21	20	7	5	3	6	6	4	6
College dean	25	21	10	11	31	23	17	23	13	22
Department chairman	7	16	5	14	12	20	6	8	18	11
College faculty	1	0	0	7	7	19	11	15	12	10
Assistant to president	1	5	0	0	5	2	2	5	0	2
Dean of students	2	0	0	4	5	3	2	1	4	3
Acting president	1	0	0	0	1	1	0	0	0	0*
Other administration	5	11	10	0	1	6	4	11	8	4
Junior college president	0	0	0	0	5	0	1	0	0	1
Public school superintendent	1	0	0	0	6	3	5	1	0	3
State Board of Education	1	0	0	0	5	0	0	0	0	1
Education Association	1	0	0	0	1	0	1	0	0	1
Other educator	1	5	0	0	2	9	3	3	0	3
Business										
President	0	0	5	0	0	0	1	0	0	1
Vice-president	0	0	0	4	0	0	1	0	4	0*
Middle management	0	0	0	4	1	0	0	0	8	1
Other										
Local-state government	2	0	0	0	2	0	0	1	0	1
Federal government	1	0	5	4	0	0	1	5	4	2
Military	0	0	0	0	0	0	0	1	9	1
Clergyman	0	..	10	0	0	..	22	1	0	8
Other	1	0	5	4	0	0	2	1	0	1
Total per cent	100	100	100	100	100	100	100	100	100	100

*Less than 0.5 per cent.

demic presidents in this study. Men who were officers in foundations represented 1 per cent of the total president group. No presidents came directly from farming occupations.

There also are variations in the prior positions held associated with the president's type of institution. Among public university presidents, the three leading positions were: college dean, 25 per cent; academic vice-president or provost, 24 per cent; and another college or university presidency, 19 per cent. By combining the two types of vice-presidents, 31 per cent moved directly from that level. Not one public university president in the sample came directly from business. The top positions among Catholic university presidents were: college dean, 21 per cent; administrative vice-president, 21 per cent; department chairman, 16 per cent; and academic vice-president, 16 per cent. Among Protestant-related and independent university presidents, the vice-president level was again an important source while a college deanship, although important, was relatively less so. As with public university presidents, the presidents of other institutions were important sources for the presidency of these private universities.

Among the public liberal arts presidents (93 per cent of whom came directly from educational positions), the college deanship clearly stood out as number one (31 per cent), followed by departmental chairman (12 per cent). Although nearly one in three public liberal arts presidents came directly from a college dean's position, the rest came directly from a great variety of educational positions. The representation among the presidents of prior experience as junior college presidents and public school superintendents is noteworthy because of its relative absence among the other presidents.

The college deanship, department chairman, and faculty member were key direct sources for the Catholic liberal arts presidents. The Protestant-related liberal arts presidents tended to come primarily from a Protestant clergyman position (22 per cent), a college dean's position (17 per cent) and a college faculty position (11 per cent). Only in the Protestant-related liberal arts group (outside of Catholic institution presidents) were clergymen so greatly selected to a presidency. This is even more striking in that no clergymen were found among the presidents of public colleges and universities.

The heads of independent liberal arts colleges came directly from a college deanship (23 per cent), college faculty (15 per cent), and an academic vice-presidency (11 per cent). Department chairmen, college deans, and academic vice-presidents were the leading sources for a technological institution presidency.

As one compares the so-called springboards to the academic presidency across the various types of institutions, the following generalizations seem evident:

(1) Academic presidents came from a variety of positions, but the majority were from the general field of education, mainly higher education. Relatively few came directly from business, government, military, or professions outside the clergy.

(2) A relatively greater percentage of university presidents came from very high level educational positions when compared to their counterparts in liberal arts colleges. In universities, few men were selected to the presidency who previously served beneath the levels of college dean, vice-president, or presidency of another institution. While these levels were important for liberal arts presidents as well, there were relatively greater numbers selected from department chairmen, faculty positions, and other educational avenues (junior colleges and public schools).

Even when the analysis of last positions held is based upon tenure in office, little differences result. Table 38 shows the comparisons for the educational positions held by presidents who have served for varying numbers of years. When the prior positions of presidents are compared with tenure in office, no significant changes in trends occur, except possibly with the academic vice-presidency. About 21 per cent of the presidents chosen last year and 15 per cent selected one to five years ago came from an academic vice-presidency, seriously rivalling the college deanship as the top current direct avenue to the presidency. When the administrative vice-presidency is added to the college deanship and academic vice-presidency, it can be seen that one-half of all the presidents selected last year held one of these three positions.

A pattern was developed indicating that presidents of public institutions were educated and later taught at primarily public institutions—while presidents of private institutions were educated and later taught at private colleges and universities. This pattern was found again when an analysis was made not only of the position held prior to the presidency but of the type of institution as well. Evidence showed that 73 per cent of public university presidents held positions in public universities; 64 per cent of Catholic univer-

TABLE 38

EDUCATIONAL POSITIONS HELD PRIOR TO PRESIDENCY

Position in Education	All Presidents 1968	Number of Years in Office					
		New	1–5	6–10	11–15	16–20	Over 20
	(per cent)	(per cent)	(per cent)	(per cent)	(per cent)	(per cent)	(per cent)
Academic president	7	3	6	10	10	5	4
Academic vice-president	11	21	15	10	7	2	7
Administrative vice-president	6	7	7	6	3	5	2
College dean	22	23	22	20	25	26	13
Department chairman	11	13	11	9	11	13	13
Faculty	10	7	10	10	9	12	18
Assistant to president	2	3	3	3	2	0	2
Public school superintendent	3	2	1	4	8	7	7
Junior college president	1	0	1	2	2	2	0
Dean of students	3	0	3	3	1	3	9
Other college administrator	4	3	5	4	4	2	7
Acting president	0*	2	0*	0	1	0	0
Education association officer	1	0	0*	0	2	2	0
State board of education officer	1	0	0*	1	2	5	2
Other education	3	3	2	4	3	2	0
Total per cent in education	85	87	86	86	90	86	84

*Less than 0.5 per cent.

sity presidents were in Catholic universities; 55 per cent of Protestant-related university presidents were in private, non-Catholic institutions; 60 per cent of independent university presidents held positions in independent universities; 43 per cent of public liberal arts presidents were previously in public liberal arts and another 23 per cent were in public universities; 81 per cent of Catholic college presidents were in Catholic colleges; 44 per cent of Protestant-related liberal arts presidents were directly from Protestant-related liberal arts colleges and universities; and 68 per cent of independent college presidents were from independent colleges. Not only did the president hold a prior position in an institution under a similar form of control (public or private), but he tended to hold a position in the same type of institution he now heads (university or liberal arts college).

Since this phase of the research aimed at determining the most direct springboards to the presidency, there was also some concern as to how long, on the average, the person held the prior position. With no real differences among presidents, it was found that the presidents held their immediately prior positions generally about five and one-half years.

Mobility is a critical concept in another sense. While we know that the majority of the presidents spent their careers in education, consideration is now given to show the mobility of these men and women between and among various educational institutions. Have they obtained their professional experiences at one institution or possibly more? Such a consideration reflects a degree of physical mobility as well as occupational mobility.

Association with
Other Colleges

To determine the extent of involvement and association with other colleges, the presidents were asked at how many different colleges or universities they held full-time faculty or administrative positions. Data in Table 39 show that, on the average, academic presidents were full-time teachers or administrative officers at nearly three colleges and universities, including their present institutions. This mean average of two other institutions (in addition to the present institution) was found among presidents of public universities, Protestant-related universities, public liberal arts colleges, and independent liberal arts colleges. The presidents of independent

TABLE 39
ASSOCIATION WITH OTHER ACADEMIC INSTITUTIONS

Presidents' Institutions	Number of Colleges or Universities Associated with, Including Present One				
	One (per cent)	Two (per cent)	Three (per cent)	Four (per cent)	Five or More (per cent)
Public university	10	29	30	15	16
Catholic university	25	50	15	5	5
Protestant-related university	14	33	19	14	20
Independent university	7	31	17	24	21
Public liberal arts	17	19	29	20	15
Catholic liberal arts	54	26	13	5	2
Protestant liberal arts	29	29	21	14	7
Independent liberal arts	16	28	23	16	17
Technological	30	23	20	13	14
Per cent for all presidents	26	27	22	14	11

universities were somewhat higher than the mean, while the presidents of Protestant-related colleges and technological institutions were somewhat below. More noticeable differences were apparent for the presidents of Catholic institutions. Among the Catholic liberal arts presidents, 54 per cent had never been a full-time staff member at an institution outside the present one, and 80 per cent had been associated with no more than one other college. The same holds for Catholic university presidents, although most had worked full-time in at least one other institution.

Even though the presidents stayed in similar types of institutions, they were indeed physically mobile as well as occupationally mobile during their full-time careers and their formal education.

Previous Administrative Experiences

As the chief academic administrator at an institution, the president must rely heavily upon his past experiences, training, knowledge, and often his intuition, in order to lead the institution most effectively. Many presidents have served in a variety of academic administrative positions and have observed, on the average, three different presidential styles of leadership at different colleges prior to their own selection. It is assumed that the administrative experiences prior to the presidency contributed (positively and negatively) to the early style adopted by the presidents as they entered their roles.

While a majority of presidents had some educational administrative experience, a number had only part-time experience and really remained teaching faculty members with different levels of administrative responsibilities. In some cases, these people are hidden in the occupational categories of "last position held" and it is difficult to know how many had full-time educational administrative experience based solely upon the position's title. A questionnaire item was inserted to obtain the additional clarification, and Table 40 gives two aspects related to their prior administrative role. First, a percentage is given to indicate how many had no full-time educational administrative experience prior to assuming the presidency, and then a mean average is given for those who have had full-time experience.

Almost one-third of the individuals now serving as academic pres-

TABLE 40
PREVIOUS ADMINISTRATIVE EXPERIENCE

Presidents' Institutions	Percentage With No Full-Time Administrative Experience	Average Number of Years Full-Time Experience
Public university	4	10.7
Catholic university	10	7.5
Protestant-related university	33	10.6
Independent university	17	10.6
Public liberal arts	20	10.5
Catholic liberal arts	49	9.4
Protestant-related liberal arts	41	10.5
Independent liberal arts	32	10.1
Technological	27	10.3
All presidents	31	10.6

idents had no full-time educational administration experience prior to assuming the presidency.

While a majority of the presidents spent significant portions of their careers in education, almost one out of three had no full-time administrative experience. For the two-thirds with prior full-time educational administrative experience, the average at all types of institutions was about ten and one-half years. Data in Table 40 give some support to the discussion of the personal reactions of many presidents as they described their careers. Several indicated that they did not choose a career in educational administration but in higher education. The presidency was largely accidental and one toward which they drifted, either unconsciously or consciously. At this point, it is seen that almost one-third of the presidents may have had strong reasons to make such statements since the presidency was in actuality their first serious full-time endeavor in educational administration, even though a career was spent in various positions in higher education.

Mobility Between Presidencies

What is the extent of mobility between presidencies of institutions in the country? How many academic presidents have been heads of other colleges and universities sometime prior to this position? About 12 per cent of the current academic presidents (that is, ninety individuals) have been presidents of other colleges or universities earlier in their careers, 10 per cent of whom have presided over one other institution and 2 per cent who have presided over two or more other institutions. (Only one person in the sample had presided over more than two other institutions, and that was three.) There are interesting variations among the different types of institutions the presidents now head. For example, most multi-institution presidents were found among public university presidents where nearly one out of four had presided over another college or university. At the other end of the continuum were Catholic liberal arts college presidents among whom only one person had presided over another institution. The other types of presidents fall in between these points as evidenced by the percentages given in Table 41. In general, it can be

TABLE 41

PRESIDENTS WHO PREVIOUSLY PRESIDED OVER OTHER INSTITUTIONS

Presidents' Institutions	Percentage Presiding Over:		
	One Other Institution	Two or More Institutions	No Other Institutions
Public university	17	7	76
Catholic university	10	0	90
Protestant-related university	10	10	80
Independent university	14	6	80
Public liberal arts	14	1	85
Catholic liberal arts	0	1	99
Protestant-related liberal arts	10	1	89
Independent liberal arts	9	0	91
Technological	0	4	96
All presidents	10	2	88

said that the career patterns of college and university presidents have proved to be more striking in their similarities than in their differences.

Very little has been said in this book about the role of academic presidents—that is, what it is they do as presidents. Although this particular study was not aimed specifically at the role of presidents, the research touched on some broad aspects of how presidents use their time. Three items in the questionnaire asked (1) the percentage of time spent in seven activities within the institution that require some involvement of the president; (2) the percentage of time spent with seven different persons or groups within or close to the institution; (3) the extent of membership in a variety of educational, business, and governmental boards of trustees (or regents, directors) that also exert special types of demands on the president.

The first role-related item in the questionnaire asked the president to rank seven specified activities in terms of the percentage of time spent in each activity during a typical month. This simple ranking scheme is fraught with obvious difficulties, but it was believed that a scheme that offered a collective and summary analysis for the rankings of all presidents might have some merit.[3] There is remarkable consistency in the perception of how time is reportedly used by the presidents.

The presidents of public and private institutions ranked their activities the same, with the exception of fund-raising activities and meetings with government officials. The public institution presidents placed governmental conferences third, while the private institution presidents in their search for many non-public sources of money and gifts, placed fund-raising third and government meetings last. It should be noted that the ranking analysis was conducted for presidents of different types of institutions, for male and female presidents, for presidents of differing tenures in office, and the rank order remained the same as above.

In order to find out how much time is spent on the two leading activities of general administration and faculty-student conferences, the presidents were also asked to indicate the percentage of time spent on the activities ranked numbers one and two. For general administration (including budget review, planning and evaluating, and policy meetings with central staff), 42 per cent of the presidents said they spent over 50 per cent of their time, while another 22 per cent of the presidents said general administration required between 35 and 50 per cent of their time. It is interesting to note that the importance and amount of time spent on general administration does not increase with the size of the institution, but is fairly consistent for all presidents. As for the activity ranked second, conferences with faculty and students, about 64 per cent of the presidents said

3. Such difficulties included: some activities that a president considers important are missing; simple ranking cannot reveal the amount of distance between each rank; what is typical one month varies with the next; what is typical to one is not typical to another; personal estimates of how time is allocated and used depends upon one's perception and awareness and may be colored by many different conditions and crises.

TABLE 42
RANKING OF TIME-CONSUMING ACTIVITIES

Activity	Rank Given by Presidents of:	
	Public Institutions	Private Institutions
General administration	1	1
Meetings with faculty, students, alumni	2	2
Meetings with state legislators	3	7
Educational activities at state and national levels	4	4
Social occasions	5	5
Meetings with business leaders	6	6
Fund-raising	7	3

that such activities required about 20 per cent of their time. It is apparent that in the eyes of the presidents, the two activities of general administration and meetings with faculty and students demand nearly three-fourths of their time.

The presidents were asked to focus on the persons or groups within the institution and to indicate the relative percentages of time spent with each in a somewhat typical week; Table 43 gives these results.

The third role-related item investigated centers upon the president's involvement in high level policy-making committees in education, business, government, and foundations. It is often heard that presidents have significant involvement in such boards, although no ready source supplies any collective data. Table 44 shows the percentage of presidents who are boards of trustee members in a variety of areas *outside* their own institutions.

TABLE 43
TIME SPENT WITH PERSONS AT INSTITUTION

Person or Group	Rank (1 = highest)	Average (mean) Per cent of Time Spent with Each
Board of Trustees	5	8
Alumni	7	6
Students	3	13
Faculty (individually or as committees)	2	20
Administrative staff	1	36
Civic leaders	4	10
Others	6	7

TABLE 44
PRESIDENTS HOLDING OUTSIDE BOARD MEMBERSHIPS

	Percentage with Board Memberships				
Area of Board Membership	*No Boards*	*One Board*	*Two Boards*	*Three Boards*	*More than Three Boards*
Another college	80	14	4	1	0*
Education Association	49	30	10	6	5
Private Foundation	69	24	5	0*	0*
Public Foundation	91	8	0*	0*	0*
Business Board	67	21	8	2	2
Government	63	25	7	2	3
Other types	76	16	4	2	2

*Less than 0.5 per cent.

Table 44 indicates that academic presidents are involved in outside policy-making boards, but the involvement varies with the type of board.

In general, the presidents of universities have relatively greater involvement in outside boards than do liberal arts college presidents. Furthermore, the type of president least likely to be a member of such boards is the Catholic liberal arts college president.

It was also considered whether relatively few presidents tend to monopolize board memberships in different areas, such as business, government, or foundations, while a fairly large percentage of presidents might actually hold no membership in any boards outside the institution. Only 9 per cent of all academic presidents are not members of a board outside their institution. Data show that 16 per cent of all presidents are members of one type of board, 24 per cent are members of two different types of boards, 24 per cent are members of three different types of boards, and 27 per cent are members of more than three different types of boards. Thus, at least one-fourth of the academic presidents do hold membership on at least four boards outside the institution, many of which are in different areas of interest.

8

Career Perceptions

The variety of data this study has revealed should not lead one to believe that these men and women chose the careers they did in a relatively simplified, mechanistic fashion. Academic presidents were asked to express their opinions and feelings about the direction and meaning of their careers; their perceptions add a valuable complement to the records they formally reflect on paper. Without such a qualitative consideration, a significant part of understanding their occupational mobility might be limited or overlooked. These individuals developed and responded to a variety of attitudes, feelings, hopes, and values as they moved along from their places of birth to the presidency.

The selection of a self-satisfying occupational career is enmeshed in a complex process which seems to be a relatively simple task for some and very difficult for others. Social scientists have long recognized the importance of factors such as family influences, education, sex-differentiation, and geographical location in the formation of values and attitudes about the world of work and careers. Edward

Gross offered a clear statement of this recognition when he stated that

persons in our culture are theoretically free to enter any occupation . . . but many factors affect the probability of entry into an occupation. Instead then of speaking of persons as *choosing* an occupation (though all may try), we find it more revealing to ask how they are selected for the occupation. This approach leads us to focus on such factors as family, location, sex, age, access to education, social class, race, and national origin.[1]

The research design for this study has been in the spirit and methodology of a sociological perspective. This is in no way to suggest that psychological factors are unimportant in occupational and career matters, but to make clear that within the purposes of this study, attention has been focused mainly on factors outside the inner psychological worlds of the academic presidents.

A discussion of the topic of occupational selection or career motivation makes necessary some understanding of the meaning of *work* in American society. Even a cursory glance at the literature indicates that work means a multitude of things to people. For example, Morse and Weiss found that work serves a means for an individual to become tied into the larger society, of having something to do, of having a purpose in life.[2] Super stated that work determines social status, molds values and sentiments, and routinizes the style of living.[3] Friedmann and Havighurst found that work often means different things to members of different occupational levels, and the higher levels are more apt to mention non-monetary factors and to stress the challenge and great purpose of their work.[4] Anne Roe some time ago noted the role of work in American society when she said ". . . there is no single situation which is potentially so capable of giving satisfaction at all levels of the basic needs as is the occupation."[5] There are numerous philosophies and theories that explain

1. Edward Gross, *Work and Society* (New York: The Thomas Crowell Company, 1958), p. 144.
2. Nancy C. Morse and R. S. Weiss, "The Function and Meaning of Work and the Job," in *Man, Work, and Society,* ed. Sigmund Nosow and William H. Form (New York: Basic Books, Inc., 1962), p. 29.
3. Donald E. Super, *The Psychology of Careers* (New York: Harper and Brothers, 1957), p. 35.
4. E. A. Friedmann and Robert J. Havighurst, "Work and Retirement," in *Man, Work, and Society,* ed. Nosow and Form, pp. 53–54.
5. Anne Roe, *The Psychology of Occupations* (New York: John Wiley and Sons, Inc., 1956), p. 31.

why people select or find themselves in the occupations they do.

The accident theory: Advocates of this school of thought usually stress the idea that individuals make decisions about future occupations accidentally, and it is therefore impossible to critically evaluate all the alternative factors. Prominent people who supposedly had found themselves accidentally in a career and excelled in it are usually mentioned to support this theory; such people, for example, as David Ricardo, Malinowski, and Whistler.[6]

Unconscious forces theory: The unconscious forces theory had its origins in the early psychological school of human behavior and motivation. Its proponents maintain that the decisions to enter a given occupation are not a result of conscious deliberation, but rather a result of latent forces which influence the individual toward a given occupation, for example, the person who manifests drives for dominance and then selects a career granting power over others' lives.[7]

Psychological theories: Advocates of psychological theories hold that "while the limits and pressures of uncontrollable external circumstances play a part, general psychological factors . . . are of major causal importance."[8] These psychological factors often emphasize the role of impulsive emotions and the satisfaction of basic needs in addition to economic gains. Many current researchers and writers have postulated a needs hierarchy beginning with physical and safety needs and moving upward to self-actualization needs. The relentless striving upward to self-actualization, to becoming all that one can become, "may well be the big factor in determining those who put enormous yet easy and pleasant effort into their work from those who do not."[9]

Developmental theories: These theories stress that the final occupational choice can be understood only in terms of the stages of development through which an individual has passed. As such, occupational choice is a developmental process, a series of decisions over a period of years that are largely irreversible and end in a compromise.[10]

6. Eli Ginzberg, Sol Ginzburg, Sidney Axelrod, and John Herman, *Occupational Choice, An Approach to a General Theory* (New York: Columbia University Press, 1951), pp. 18–19.
7. Ibid., pp. 21–22.
8. Bertram R. Faier, "Personality Factors in Occupational Choice," *Educational Psychological Measurement*, 13 (1953), 362.
9. Roe, *Psychology of Occupations*, p. 33.
10. Ginzberg et al, *Occupational Choice*, pp. 186–98.

It is not the purpose here to discuss the merits and limitations of each of these approaches and theories; they have been set forth simply to show that any discussion of why academic presidents (or any group) chose their present positions is a complex and weighty task, subject to a variety of interpretations.

Views expressed by the academic presidents in this study serve as a comprehensive report on how their career decisions of the past and present look to them at the present time. Their remarks, then, are "time-bound." In a few years from now, their views might change, while a few years ago they might have given different views. This chapter looks at the presidents' career decisions after they attained their positions and while they are still in them. Because there is a complete dependence upon the personal perceptions and reactions of the respondents, any of the weaknesses of self-appraisals and how they might relate to one's self-concept are inherent in the approach. In view of the candor and obvious effort involved in most of the written statements and personal interviews, there is good reason to believe that the presidents were quite open and willing to react honestly to the question of why they chose academic administration. It is assumed that their conscious responses provide a greater insight into and understanding of the substantial appearance of their career lines.

A number of career-related factors were identified following a content analysis of nearly 400 questionnaire responses, and these factors were used to organize the personal remarks. Fundamental reasons for following careers in higher educational administration can be classified by six interrelated factors: (1) a service orientation, (2) social influences, (3) professional opportunities, (4) personal factors, (5) a developmental process, and (6) an accidental circumstance. In most cases one or more of the six factors interrelated in the eventual career decision; at other times, the respondents were most likely to insist that one had an overpowering influence.

Alternative Careers Considered

The presidents were asked this question: *"From the time you completed your undergraduate education until the present, had you ever seriously considered a career outside the context of an educational institution?"* They were asked to check, if applicable, one or

more of the listed occupational alternatives. Six out of ten presidents
indicated that they had seriously considered a career outside education from the time they completed their college education to the
present, as shown in Table 45. The independent university presidents, Protestant-related college presidents, and technological institution presidents were much more likely to have considered another
career, while the Catholic institution presidents were least likely.
The tabulation is given in Table 46 for those who answered affir-
matively in Table 45, and the career alternatives are delineated.

TABLE 45
PRESIDENTS WHO CONSIDERED ANOTHER CAREER

Presidents' Institutions	Percentage Answering:	
	Yes	No
Public university	63	37
Catholic university	50	50
Protestant-related university	60	40
Independent university	90	10
Public liberal arts	59	41
Catholic liberal arts	28	72
Protestant-related liberal arts	74	26
Independent liberal arts	59	41
Technological	84	16
All presidents	60	40

It can be seen that 29 per cent of the presidents who had seriously
considered other careers were oriented toward religious service, the
most-mentioned outside career.[11]

About 18 per cent of the presidents seriously considered business
careers, 9 per cent government service, and another 12 per cent
considered careers in both business and government. (Thus, a total
of 39 per cent considered alternative careers in business or government.) Approximately 16 per cent of the presidents considered private practice in a professional field such as law, medicine, and engineering. About 2 per cent saw the military as a desirable alternative,
and less than 0.5 per cent seriously considered labor union careers.

11. It should be pointed out that this figure includes 10 per cent who were priests,
nuns, or Protestant ministers already. Thus, if this group were removed, it would
mean that 19 per cent of the presidents who were not now clergymen had considered
careers in religious service. The 19 per cent would still be the top career alternative,
but would be closer to those who considered other careers.

TABLE 46
ALTERNATIVE CAREERS CONSIDERED

Alternative Career	Percentage of Respondents
Business executive	18
Government	9
Business and government careers	12
Religious service	29
Labor union official	0*
Military officer	2
Practicing professional (law, medicine, engineering, and others)	16
Other occupations	14
Total per cent	100

*Less than 0.5 per cent.

It has been noted that very few presidents in this study actually tried occupations outside education. The central question now asked is "why?" Why did most academic presidents spend the very large portion of their full-time careers in education as opposed to any other career? More specifically, what factors, values, philosophies, or forces contributed to the decisions of these individuals to make their way in education when many of society's more tangible rewards seem to go to leaders in business and government? Why did few actually work full time in business or government when many seriously considered a career in business or government? Why did some leave teaching positions in higher education for the administrative area, the latter having more burdens and creating more demands than faced by many as college professors?

Career Motivations

A minority of academic presidents said they chose academic administration and the presidency, irregardless of the type, size, or location of the institution or tenure of the president. The presidents are most likely to say they were chosen or selected, but they "did not choose."[12] A majority of academic presidents believe they were

12. The question which brought out this aspect was the final questionnaire item asking why they "chose" academic administration. After the pilot test, it was obvious that the question made respondents react to the word "chose"—positively or negatively—and for this reason was retained with no modifications.

chosen by religious superiors or by trustees who felt they could do the job, or by a set of unique circumstances. For most, higher education administration was not their career at all, but rather higher education. For many, during the course of their careers in higher education (primarily as teachers and deans), they were asked to assume enlarged responsibilities in educational administration, including the presidency. Many of these men expressed reluctance to accept the presidency at that time, but they felt unable to turn down the request. Once in the position, they remained for a number of reasons, personal philosophies, and institutional necessities.

The study identified a number of presidents who admit having made an active career choice in higher educational administration with the ambition of becoming president. Whether presidents perceive their presence in their positions mainly as a matter of active choice, as acceptance to the wishes of others, or for some other reasons, there are a variety of rationales expressed. The most expressed reason probably is "service."

Service Orientation

Service is a popularly articulated concept of academic presidents, and it took at least four major forms: to God and church, to society, to higher education, and to the institution.

Service to God and church. Although many presidents speak of service to God, the majority of such expressions come from the heads of Catholic and Protestant-related institutions.

The following are typical responses from Catholic institution presidents telling why these men and women chose the careers they did.

> *As a Catholic priest I did not choose educational administration, but was requested to take the presidency by my religious superior.*

> *The headship of this institution was assigned to me by the Bishop of the diocese without my asking it.*

> *As a member of a religious order, I have not chosen educational administration, but was appointed to the position. I was given an option, of course, and agreed to the appointment.*

I chose administration in higher education as a career because I am a member of the Jesuits, and higher education is one of our principal works.

For a large percentage of Catholic college and university presidents, their association with education is integral to their membership in a religious community. They are most likely to indicate that they responded to requests and wishes (and in some cases, assignments) of their religious superiors. Their careers as priests or nuns and educators have been interwined.

The presidents of Protestant-related institutions (many of whom are clergymen) are also likely to stress service to God and church when speaking of their careers:

Ours is a church college, service here is really one form of church service. I felt guided by God to become president of this institution.

I spent many years as a minister prior to becoming president of ——— college. The position has been challenging and gratifying. I hope my service has been helpful. I do not feel that I left the Christian ministry, I simply enlarged and extended it.

As one who believes that all human beings have been created as an expression of divine purpose, I have always felt a strong feeling of having a mission in higher education.

My basic reason for accepting the position came from my conviction of the importance of the church-related liberal arts college and its unique contribution to a total system of higher education in America.

I accepted the position because of a growing conviction that I could render my greatest service to God and man in this assignment.

It is a combination of the significance of the work and one's fitness for doing it. I am committed wholeheartedly to the Christian liberal arts college as an essential ingredient in human society. I regard what I am doing more as a "calling" than a job. It is what I was meant to do.

For many of the presidents of Protestant-related colleges, a predominant theme is one of service to God, the church, and a particular commitment to a type of educational institution. The presidency represents more of a "calling" reminiscent of the values articulated by presidents of early colleges in America and continued through the traditions and objectives of many of these institutions today. The presidency has provided an enlarged ministry, an opportunity to serve people in a larger sense than that offered by most pastorates. Therefore, when approached by a board of control or faculty committee about the presidency, these presidents largely welcomed the opportunity.

Service to society. Service to society and to one's fellowman is an often-voiced comment by presidents in all types of institutions:

> *Man is born to serve and this is an excellent position within and from which service can be rendered.*

> *Basically, I have a deep conviction that I have a responsibility to other men for service. This basic drive, along with a love for young people, makes the academic setting attractive. The opportunity to further the cause was made available in administration.*

> *Having embarked on a career as a college teacher, I came to the conclusion that I would make more of a contribution to education in administration than in teaching. The job of being a college president is tough, exciting, and rewarding, its decisions less simple than those of teaching, its pressures much greater. No doubt in some subtle sense the awareness of power provides additional satisfaction, though I would like to believe that the opportunity of service has been more important in my case. Who knows himself well enough to be sure.*

Service to higher education. Service in the interest of higher education itself is an important theme for academic presidents:

> *I am a strong supporter of higher education and top university administration is a more effective* shot *[sic] from which to provide leadership and service to bring about change in higher education.*

My choice of education was partly a process of elimination but, most important, it was based upon a growing conviction that man's problems could only be resolved in the long run through self-improvement by education. I preferred the idea of higher education both because the atmosphere was more appealing and challenging and also because I felt service at that level had to deal with the real potential of man in terms of his higher intellect in abstract reasoning. . . . Higher education is the most important social force by which man can raise himself by his own bootstraps.

Higher education is one of the most meaningful undertakings of these times. Administrative roles make possible accomplishments denied less general responsibilities.

I think education, particularly higher education, holds the key to most of our national and international problems today. Thus, it offers great opportunity for public service.

Service to an institution. The other major concept of service expressed by college and university presidents is service to an institution. It has been noted that many presidents are alumni of their present institutions; these men in particular felt strongly about returning to serve their alma mater. Others who were faculty members and staff members at the institution or who were chosen to render assistance to a college that was having serious difficulties or was approaching some distinction, are leading candidates to talk about serving the institution:

I am a researcher who accepted my present position only because I felt that I had something to contribute to the growth of my alma mater. I would not have accepted the post elsewhere.

I chose a career in administration in higher education as opposed to any other career because it gave me an opportunity to serve an institution and a cause, both of which are very dear to me.

I left my prior position and came to ———, more because of my admiration of the institution than of any preference for administration over research and teaching.

The challenge of returning in an administrative capacity to the institution from which I graduated was a stimulating factor.

As a student and faculty member early in my career at this institution, I had gratifying years. When invited by the trustees to return I was aware that the university needed strengthening and thought it would be interesting to see what I could do to that end.

I accepted the position as president mainly because of deep loyalty to the university and a deep sense of gratitude for the education I received from it.

For the presidents who felt deeply about the future of their institutions for a number of reasons, their career decisions tended to be expressed in terms of serving that institution, more so than higher education or society, although these latter aspects would ultimately be strengthened.

Service to God and church, to society and man, to higher education, and to an institution or type of institution are important elements of many presidents' career decisions. The idea of service was often rooted in family upbringings where for many, a professional life was in a sense nurtured. But others have felt the commitment to service from religious ties, deep feelings for an institution, and the possible contributions to the society.

Social Influences

Many presidents speak of associations with key persons whom they believed to have played a crucial role in their career decisions. Family, friends, colleagues, and teachers were "significant others" in the lives of these individuals and led them directly or indirectly to develop certain attitudes and values toward education and higher education administration.

In a few cases, racial concerns were part of the mix that led to the presidency.

I grew up in a family in which service was oriented to higher education and selected this area because of that orientation and interest.

I didn't know any better—my father did it too!

I was reared in a home in which my father served successively as teacher, principal, and superintendent by the time I went to college. I enjoyed my life in that "schoolman's" home and looked forward to earning a livelihood one day in a comparable setting. I have never really known any other kind of life.

I have been fortunate in having the opportunity to work closely with some outstanding college presidents. They inspired me to what was possible with the presidency.

My interest in higher education administration was originally aroused by two professors from whom I took courses in educational administration at ——— University. Their encouragement to pursue graduate work in educational administration confirmed my determination to work in this field.

It had always been assumed that if I didn't become a doctor like my father, I'd become a college president like his father. This was gentle pressure but played a role, I am sure.

As a Negro there were a limited number of opportunities available in seeking a career . . . education offered more than any other area of endeavor. If there had been other professional choices available, it is more likely that I would not have entered education.

Though it sounds immodest, I have a sense of noblesse oblige *probably inculcated by my family, which has a tradition of civic leadership. My father once said to me, "if you are asked to perform a difficult job worth doing, and you can do it, then you must do it."*

Thus, in many cases, values and aspirations and strong influences affecting the career were supplied by key people at different life stages. There is little question, but the family and teachers were significant in influencing many presidents to begin a career in education and eventually move to higher education administration and the presidency.

Professional Opportunities

A number of aspects that directly relate to the position, role, and professional opportunities associated with the academic presidency are seen as attractions that led a number of these men and women into educational administration. Some of these aspects are tangible—such as salary, home, and a certain standard of living. However, most references are made to more intangible aspects such as satisfactions, challenges, and frustrations afforded by academic administration.

> *I accepted the challenge of the presidency because I thought I could affect the lives of a greater number of people. . . . I also thought the presidency presented in one package the "complete" challenge to all that a man had. It was dangerous; it was costly; it was adventuresome; it was exhausting; and yet it was refreshing and invigorating. It was an adequate substitute for total war!*

> *The reason I selected higher education administration was the life that centers around a campus, both intellectual and social. To be an administrator is to be in the "eye" of the storm! I enjoy it.*

> *The main reason is the challenge of developing and running one's own institution while correlating at the same time ideas and needs of the board members, faculty, students, alumni, and the local community.*

> *It is useful and productive, and it is somewhat less cutthroat than business and more useful than many businesses.*

> *It is more fun.*

> *I entered administration because I felt there was a greater challenge than that found in the classroom. A career in any other field comparable to that of higher education would undoubtedly have to be pursued in a larger area.*

> *Academic administration was quite frankly an attractive alternative to professorial "publish or perish" pressures.*

*I enjoy working with people of college age and academic ad-
ministration offered continuing contact in a larger sense than
that possible in the classroom.*

*I shifted to academic administration because it provided me
with a generalist perspective of an institution, rather than a
limited focus of the typical faculty member.*

*I enjoy the challenge of applying theories and principles of the
ivory tower to the realities of the market-place.*

*The salary of top administrators is better than straight teach-
ing and the economic rewards enable me to live at the level and
style I prefer. There is also greater prestige.*

*I enjoy being where the action is, like being one of the barons of
the realm within the educational establishment.*

*There are very few professions that challenge the intellect,
courage, and energy as does administration in higher education. It is a period of unrest and uncertainty, but it offers a
challenge to the administrator who is not just interested in the
status quo.*

Job-oriented elements rank very high among the reasons why presidents chose their careers. Although many speak of the disadvantages
of the positions, most feel the presidency is worth the effort because
of relatively more advantages. A number of presidents feel strongly
that "the pressures upon top college administrators today, are most
frustrating, continuing, and increasing. The challenges are no longer
worth the toll." Some of these pressures are pinpointed by the following concern:

*The current trend for faculty and students to demand more
decision-making will lead to an even greater exodus of administrators from the scene. To be held responsible without the
authority to make the decisions is asking the impossible. I am
not referring to academic decisions but to the overall general
administrative decisions required in any large organization.*

There is little question that the contemporary presidents are beset by numerous pressures, as are all high level administrators in organized society, but only a minority (based upon their statements) feel that the pressures are more exacting than the opportunities, challenges, or excitement associated with the position.[13]

In the eyes of a majority of presidents, the position gives status, adequate financial compensation, and makes possible a style of living preferred by the presidents and their families. The work is seen as "trying" and yet most felt it stimulating to be at the center of the various campus publics. A few indicated they are suffering from "presidential fatigue" and look forward to returning to the classroom. And a few expressed the belief that a president gives his best to the presidency within ten years and thereafter should shift or withdraw.

Very closely tied to the professional-oriented elements are those that rest with the president as a person.

Personal Factors

Personal factors include the psychological or inner ideals, drives, and ambitions of the presidents involved in this study. Based upon their comments given in preceding sections, one is able to obtain a general impression of the types of persons they must be, and yet a large percentage offered more specific ideas about themselves as human beings that they believed had some place in their decisions to enter academic administration.

I accepted the position largely as a dare. I was clearly too young and inexperienced for the job, but I wanted to see if I could make it as top man.

---

13. There seemed to be some indication that those with the longer tenures as faculty members and longer tenures as presidents were more apt to speak of the disadvantages and frustrations of the position—supporting the New York study by Hemphill—but since the question was open-ended no correlations could be made without an amount of bias that might have distorted the results. On the other hand, some of the most articulate spokesmen who had only the most praiseworthy comments about the presidency were often those with relatively long faculty and presidential tenures.

I am competitive by nature and I like to be the "head man" in whatever group I am. However, there are many other conscious and sub-conscious motivations, but perhaps not the least of these is like the mountain climber's answer, "Because it's there."

I believe my personal motivations were quite pure, though adulterated somewhat by ego and personal ambition, I suspect.

I shifted to administration because I had certain aptitudes and a temperament conducive to administrative activities.

I preferred to be a manager in education because a smoothly running organization appeals to me, as does a machine that runs efficiently and smoothly.

I enjoy making things move, releasing energy in others for constructive ends.

It is the thing that interests me the most. I understand the problems and have dedicated myself to the premise that they can be solved and that I can solve them.

I enjoy having the opportunity to put into effect some of my ideas. I miss the classroom, genuinely, not merely conventionally and sentimentally; I envy the publishing scholar; I am tortured by guilt over work always piling up faster than I can attend to it to my satisfaction, and I chafe over my own mistakes and limitations though I believe I project the appearance of confidence and poise.

I put money where my mouth is—the only way educational change can be carried out is to have college presidents ready and able to risk and to dare.

In most cases, the presidents appear to be men with a flair for making things happen; although many admit to envying the life of the scholar, these men by and large turned from such a life to accept a life of pressures peculiar to the modern administrator. Although the majority feel they were chosen with little or no serious plans to become a president as such, nearly all are ready to admit that a desire to achieve at a high level of leadership is part of their decision. They all express (with varying degrees of humility) that they had the necessary ability, sufficient confidence, and a philosophy of education that just needed to be heard and felt to warrant acceptance of the presidency. Some are quite practical about their personal motives while others take a more philosophical stance; some, like the person quoted below, combine the perspectives:

> *I believe one tries to do what one believes he does best. I like administration because I do it well—better than I could do anything else. I prefer educational administration because I like the academic environment, the general life of the community. But again, I am most familiar with the academic life; I feel most at home with it and those who pursue it. If this appears fatalistic—or even worse—not at all an inspirational reason for an academic career, charge it off to an honest attempt to be as analytical as possible about one's work, and even more basic, about one's self.*

It is interesting to note that about 25 per cent of the presidents stated they are in higher education administration because of (1) a series of career decisions which they believe to be rooted in accident, or (2) a set of circumstances at a point in time, or (3) as the end of a progressively deeper commitment to administration over a range of years. For all these presidents, it is an event or a process especially difficult for them to explain. The following categories attend to their interrelated perceptions, first as a developmental process over a period of years, and second as a complete accident often at a point in time.

Developmental Process

Many presidents believe their full-time movement and involvement in academic administration was almost inevitable given their interests and tendency to become more active in administrative problems early in their careers as teachers. Often they drifted in at first and occasionally they planned to enter, but once in they found it increasingly difficult to leave even when they might have wanted to. A series of career decisions largely irreversible was set in motion, according to the presidents, and almost "as fate decreed," an academic presidency, not surprisingly, was offered. The patterns of upward mobility in the higher education hierarchy are reinforced by these remarks:

It was a gradual encirclement as administrative duties began to infringe upon teaching time leading to the decision to move full-time into administration. An invitation to assume the presidency seemed inevitable once I became a dean.

I actually only consciously planned to be a college professor, but a number of proposals to assume larger and broader responsibilities led to administration. I became a university president not by planning for it, but looking backward it is easy to see that a succession of experiences led to it.

My involvement with people in learning situations led to administration in higher education, and then step by step, the job chose me.

Educational administration had an appeal from the time I first tried it as a department head. One job led to another. Subconsciously, perhaps, I always subscribed to the oft quoted idea that "the job seeks the man" in education.

I had not planned to be a college president. I did not really want to be one. I chose to do it because it seemed finally so natural to do on a larger scale what I had done in a department.

It is difficult to explain—it simply evolved.

Like Topsy, I grew into it as faculty member, dean of students, assistant to the president, academic vice-president, and then president.

My early career choice was really to teaching. But apparently my sounding off in faculty meetings and willingness to serve on committees brought on a kind of inevitable reaction. I was asked to be dean of men, then dean of the college, then president.

I doubt if very many people ever started out with the ambition of becoming a college president. If so, they should be put away. In my own case, it was a chain of circumstances of increased responsibilities in administration that led to it.

In nostalgic moments, I sometimes wonder about the path I followed (teacher, department head, dean, and president). I cannot go back now—the bridges behind me have either crumpled from disuse or have been bombed out by the revolution that now surrounds me.

My progression upward from teacher to president seemed logical a few years ago. At the present time, the wisdom of those "logical" decisions is in doubt.

I moved from teaching into academic administration by quite natural and easy stages.

From the thoughts of the presidents we have quoted their move to the presidency seemed to have had a fair amount of logic and also an inevitability about it. Very closely related are persons whose perceptions are also based upon a series of circumstances that culminated in the offer and acceptance of a presidency. But this latter group does not speak of logic and in place of inevitability; the term accident is most often used.

Accidental Circumstance

Although the stages of teacher-to-department-head-to-dean-to-president were followed by many of these individuals, they insist that each career movement was accidental, especially the presidency, and they did not entertain seriously the idea that a presidency was inevitable or a likely pattern. In addition, those who came to the presidency from outside higher education are likely to mention a circumstance or accidental happenstance that brought them to the post. Those who expressed their career choice specifically as an accident or a simple response to circumstances did so as follows:

For fifteen years I was in religious work and I never considered higher educational administration until two years ago when the board approached me about the presidency.

My eventual career in higher education administration is best explained as a roll of the dice.

It was a sheer accident and circumstance. If women are wanted, there is a very small field from which to select.

The choice was never really deliberate. I'm a drifter and there was a place for me in educational administration.

Like many other academicians, I simply "found" myself in educational administration even though I had not originally aimed at it.

Getting to the presidency was not really an accident, but a series of accidents.

I simply drifted into educational administration.

It just happened, and I sometimes wish it could have been otherwise.

Being approached about the presidency was a great surprise to me because in all my planning, I had never thought I would make my career in college administration.

My career in education would really appear to have been brought about by default rather than by design. I cannot remember a time when I thought of myself as a college dean or a college president. The job opportunities that opened appeared to be more by accident than by design.

I have had considerable experience in military service and business. I am in my present position as a result of circum-

stances and experiences. I enjoy the work but I would be equally pleased with any of the others.

Among those who felt they did not *choose* educational administration, but rather were chosen by accident or circumstance, one president offered a statement that summed up his own feelings and was indicative of the attitudes of many of the respondents:

I doubt if many people choose administration in higher education as a conscious deliberate career choice. It is something which happens to a person, like having twins or getting the mumps. It is, of course, possible to prevent it from happening by taking precautions; but it is not nearly so easy to take actions which will cause it to happen. I believe I am a college president because of a set of circumstances which are not likely to be duplicated elsewhere. It has something to do with an attitude developed over a career as a teacher in higher education and perhaps much more due to accidents of being in a particular position at a particular time.

Discussion and Summary

Motivations underlying career choices are complex and often subtle in their origin, intensity, and effects. Sometimes they seem very reasonable and clear and sometimes they are slightly irrational and vague. Sometimes they seem to be fully and carefully made, but often they are rooted in the unconscious.

In our society, a man's occupation often has great meanings which not only reflect his interests and abilities, but often his values and commitments. It offers a level or position of status and security and provides an essential part of how a man defines who he is. The relevant literature would suggest that career choices are not easily nor simply made, nor are they based upon easily explainable motives. To ask a man to explain his career choices and to expect the exact picture is fraught with shortcomings. He himself may not really know—and even if he does, he may for various reasons attempt to conceal his motivations from an outsider. Accidental factors, unconscious forces, social influences, psychological elements, and decision making over time have all been found important in different occupational choices or selections for a variety of career patterns.

Most academic presidents perceive their career patterns to be based upon one or more of the following factors: (1) a service orientation, (2) social influences, (3) professional opportunities, (4) personal factors, (5) a developmental process, and (6) an accident. It was found that few presidents see themselves as actually having *chosen* a career in higher education administration (although they admit that it could have been avoided). Most of the presidents believe it more properly-stated to refer to themselves as educators in higher education; they feel that through a series of activities and decisions, and based upon particular values, philosophies, opportunities, needs, and circumstances, they were chosen or selected to head an institution of higher education.

For some, their careers have had a sense of inevitability. They were brought up in educational or professional-oriented families and developed a sense of service at an early age. They had it nurtured and were provided models of a life of scholarship in their formal education; and they planned careers as educators. Over a period of years, they were called upon to help solve administrative problems in academic committees and departments. Experience and visibility were part of such involvement along with the commitment to education and academic administration as useful and worthy of a man's attention and energy. After experience as a dean or provost, they were called upon to assume the presidency, and for these men, the decision could be nothing but yes.

On the other hand, a number of presidents began their careers with the full expectation of religious service. Among the Catholic institution presidents a desire to teach led to candidacy and acceptance in religious orders that had major responsibilities for education. Demonstration of educational administrative abilities that came to the attention of a religious superior and an evaluation of the church's needs made possible their movement to the presidency—where the church and the institution could be served simultaneously. Among many Protestant-related institution presidents, an early career in the ministry led to work and visibility in the church's colleges. A deep commitment to the value of Christian higher education and a desire to enlarge one's ministry through academic administration made such a career move desirable for the institution and the person. And for those who were not ministers, they still shared a strong commitment to the value of a Christian college or university and this commitment made acceptance of a presidency imperative.

Some presidents came from more humble social origins and many of them began their careers as teachers, often at the elementary or secondary levels. Soon they were principals and superintendents, and they earned doctorates in educational administration, many teaching such courses at the college level. The presidency became a reality even though few anticipated earlier in their careers achieving such a position.

A few presidents spent substantial portions of their careers in business, government, or the military. Careers in academic administration had never been a part of their thinking until circumstances precipitated their selection.

It has been seen that the majority of presidents have expressed feelings of great rewards and satisfactions from the position, while some seem frustrated by the increasing pressures and more abundant demands the position and role continue to bring.

The presidents were eager to include opinions on another aspect of the academic presidency that is worthy of note. In giving their own career perceptions and feelings about the position, a relatively large number also volunteered opinions of the type of president needed in the academic presidency in the next ten years. Many of their remarks were prompted by a questionnaire item that asked for their ranking of which of the following three often-quoted characteristics of presidents is most essential: (1) the president must be above all a scholar in his own right with a notable background in teaching and research; (2) the president must be one who has demonstrated successful executive and administrative abilities in educational administration, and (3) the president must be one with considerable knowledge and training in business or financial matters related to institutional growth and development.

There was little question among all academic presidents that the contemporary and future academic president must possess, above all, educational administration talents. It should be pointed out that the size of the institution in no way changed the percentages as shown in Table 47. One president indicated in an interview that he believed it desirable for a college president to have faculty experience only because it would make him more accepted by the faculty members. Although business or financial skills were deemed impor-

TABLE 47

OPINIONS ON BACKGROUND EXPERIENCE

Background Experience Most Needed	Percentage of Presidents
The president must be a notable scholar	18
The president must be a successful educational administrator	68
The president must have business administration experience and skills	14
Total per cent	100

tant for fund-raising or general budgetary purposes, one respondent felt it was probably more important for the president to hire a trust-worthy development man and business manager. The president would be effective to the extent that he brought together and utilized well a team of competent staff members as he gave the most crucial leadership to educational goals and philosophy. Other presidents offered a range of ideas about the ideal president. The following are excerpts from their written comments:

The president must be a person who enjoys the responsibility of making decisions, both routine and the higher decisions that must be made; he must be one who is willing and enjoys inserting his ideas and projects into the mainstream of the life of the institution; he must be one who has the ability and desire to work with persons from the lowliest staff members to the highest paid professor.

The president must have intimate and extensive knowledge of modern American universities from first-hand experience. He must have high standards for people and their performance in the educational functions of a university. He must have personal enthusiasm for the institution and devotion to its purposes and its personnel and ability to communicate these characteristics to others.

To my mind, the day of the outstanding scholar being president of a university is over—it's a practical, business-oriented agency. This may well be shocking to the scholar but it is true as I view the matter.

Above all, the president must have patience, tact, courage, integrity, common sense, and good judgment.

Lord help the college presidents of the future. They will have to made of sterner stuff, and I don't consider myself any "softie."

The presidency is basically a management position and requires much the same qualities which are represented in the management of any large organization. The one peculiarity is that one seems to need a background as an ex-scholar in order to be fully acceptable to the faculty.

It is to be hoped that his motives are pure, his judgment reasonably sound, and his fundamental attitude one of humility.

The president today must receive formal training in educational administration or business administration.

Being a college president is a tough job but it can be most rewarding. Extremely sensitive people should avoid such a position, however, as we get quite a beating sometimes and can't afford to bleed too much. One has to be a master at the art of compromise and has to remember that at various times in his tenure he will be called too weak and at other times too overbearing.

9

Career Comparisons

Extensive research on the careers of big business leaders and federal executives provided the theoretical and methodological underpinning for this study of academic presidents. The findings are now compared with other related studies in order to bring into sharp relief the similarities and differences in the careers of leaders in three powerful and prestigious occupational categories in American society. Further generalizations are made about the extent to which the society is fluid or rigid in its filling of key positions in business, government, and higher education administration. To continue by following the basic format of this book, we ask: How do the occupational origins of the leaders compare? Do they come from different occupational levels? How do their geographical origins and sizes of hometowns compare? How does the formal educational preparation of the elites compare, especially at the college level? How do selected critical points related to the career lines of business, government, and educational leaders compare?[1]

1. Comparative findings in this chapter have been taken variously from three sources that have reported Warner's research: (1) W. Lloyd Warner and James C. Abegglen, *Occupational Mobility in American Business and Industry* (Minneapolis: University

TABLE 48
OCCUPATIONAL ORIGINS OF LEADERS IN THREE CATEGORIES

Occupation of Father	1952 Business Leaders		1959 Federal Executives		1968 Academic Presidents	
	Per cent	*Rank*	*Per cent*	*Rank*	*Per cent*	*Rank*
Unskilled or semiskilled laborer	5	7	4	8	6	7
Skilled laborer	10	4	17	2–3	10	4–5
Clerk, salesman	8	6	9	6	5	8
Foreman	3	8	5	7	7	6
Major executive and large business owner	31	1	17	2–3	10	4–5
Owner of small business	18	2	14	4–5	11	3
Professional	14	3	19	1	31	1
Farmer	9	5	14	4–5	16	2
Other occupations	2	9	1	9	4	9

As indicated in Table 48, nearly one-third of the fathers of business leaders were also major executives and owners of large businesses; and 14 per cent were professional men. Another 10 per cent were skilled laborers, 9 per cent were farmers, and 8 per cent were clerks or salesmen. At the lowest levels, 5 per cent of the fathers were unskilled laborers and 3 per cent were foremen. Thus, the business leaders come in large proportions from what are usually perceived as the higher occupational levels in the society, as 63 per cent of their fathers were major executives, owners of large and small businesses and professional men.

About 19 per cent of the fathers of federal executives were professional men followed closely by fathers who were major executives (17 per cent) and skilled laborers (17 per cent). Owners of small businesses and farmers are next with 14 per cent, and at the lower levels are fathers who were clerks or salesmen (9 per cent), foremen (5 per cent), unskilled laborers (4 per cent), and other occupations (1 per cent). About 50 per cent of the government leaders' fathers were

of Minnesota Press, 1955); (2) W. Lloyd Warner, Paul P. Van Riper, Norman H. Martin, and Orvis F. Collins, *The American Federal Executive* (New Haven: Yale University Press, 1963): and (3) W. Lloyd Warner, "The Careers of American Business and Government Executives: A Comparative Analysis," in *Social Science Approaches to Business Behavior,* ed. by George B. Strother (Homewood, Illinois: Richard D. Irwin, Inc., 1962). Although the researches cover different time periods, the central notion of comparative career mobility to high levels is believed valid. The evidence from current sources indicates such vertical mobility is increasing rather than decreasing.

major executives, business owners, and professionals, while about 21 per cent were skilled or unskilled laborers.

The occupational origins of academic presidents are quite similar in general terms to the other leaders in that the higher occupational levels are well-represented. About 31 per cent of the academic presidents' fathers were professional men (note that 31 per cent of business leaders' fathers were major executives). About one-half that many were farmers (16 per cent), and about 11 per cent of the fathers were major executives and another 10 per cent of the fathers were foremen, 6 per cent were unskilled laborers, 5 per cent were clerks or salesmen, and 4 per cent were in other occupations. Thus, about 52 per cent of the fathers of academic presidents were either major executives, business owners, or professional men.

Ratios were developed which permitted exact comparisons of the occupations of the presidents' fathers with the adult male population at the time the academic presidents started their careers. A ratio of 1.00 meant that the same percentage of an occupation was represented among the fathers of the educators as found in the general population. Warner also developed such ratios, and Table 49 brings them together for all three types of leaders. The data show that the occupational origins overrepresented among all leaders are business executives, business owners, professional men and foremen. The occupational levels underrepresented are clerks or salesmen, skilled laborers (except for fathers of government leaders), farmers,

TABLE 49

PROPORTIONAL REPRESENTATION RATIOS FOR THREE ELITES.

OCCUPATIONS OF ALL FATHERS

Father's Occupation	Business Leaders	Government Executives	Academic Presidents
Executive or large business owner	7.75	5.67	2.00
Owner of small business	3.60	2.00	2.20
Professional man	3.50	4.75	6.20
Foreman	1.33	2.50	2.50
Clerk, salesman	0.80	0.75	0.38
Skilled laborer	0.63	1.13	0.71
Farmer	0.45	0.88	0.73
Unskilled laborer	0.16	0.12	0.19

NOTE: The 1920 census was used for the 1952 business leader study; the 1930 census was used for the 1959 government executive study; and the 1940 census was used for the 1968 academic president study. Thus, all percentages for the adult male population have been adjusted for the appropriate time periods under investigation.

and unskilled laborers. Among the business leaders the proportional representation ratio for fathers who were major business executives was 7.75, for federal executives the ratio is 5.67. In the case of academic presidents the most overrepresented category is that of the professional man with a ratio of 6.20.

Compared with the general population, most fathers of business, government, and academic leaders have tended to come in disproportionately high numbers from the business executives or business owner levels or from professional fields. However, there was occupational movement up from the lower levels as well, although somewhat lower than might be expected. The level of foreman stands out as the only level below the top three which had a proportionally higher ratio than would be anticipated. The foreman level has been an important occupational origin for all leaders, especially government and academic leaders.

The fathers of business, government, and educational leaders who were in the professions compared to fathers in the professions within the adult male population show other contrasts. In Table 50, it is seen that among all elites the proportional ratios for the sons of lawyers, engineers, and physicians are quite similar, while the ratios for the clergyman and educator professions give noticeable differences.

Business leaders whose fathers were professors rank last with a 1.89 ratio. For government leaders the data are broken down into categories of professors: the rank of teachers is the lowest of the professions with 2.25, while college professors are very high with 14.17. Among academic presidents' origins, the categories of teacher and college professor are relatively much higher, with ratios of 23.75 and 5.54 respectively. Thus, while the teacher category is lowest for

TABLE 50
PROPORTIONAL REPRESENTATION RATIOS FOR THREE ELITES:
FATHERS IN PROFESSIONS

Profession	Business Leader	Federal Executive	Academic President
Lawyer	8.00	8.44	5.80
Clergyman	5.48	6.67	28.46
Engineer	4.80	4.77	3.63
Physician	4.78	5.95	3.91
Elementary-secondary teacher	1.89	2.25	23.75
College professor and college president		14.17	5.54

business and government executives, it is second highest for academic presidents. In the other professional category of clergyman, the academic presidents stand far ahead with the percentage of fathers who were ministers. Ministers are second for business and government executives with ratios of 5.48 and 6.67 respectively, but among academic presidents, the ratio is almost five times as great, or 28.46, and the clergyman group is the most overrepresented among the occupational origins of college and university presidents.

Geographical Origins

Academic presidents are more representative of the general population on the basis of region of birth than is the case for business or government leaders, as shown in Table 51. None of the academic presidents' regions of birth are far from a perfect representation of 1.00 (although the Middle Atlantic region is slightly under with 0.87, and the Pacific with 0.81). On the other hand, the geographical origin of the business and government leaders are disproportionately low for the southern regions. Another aspect of geographical origins studied was the relative size of the hometowns of the leaders.

As the figures show in Table 52, it is more likely for business and government leaders to come from urban areas, especially from communities over 100,000 people, while academic presidents come from the relatively smaller urban areas under 100,000 population and from rural communities under 2,500. In many respects, the

TABLE 51
PROPORTIONAL REPRESENTATION RATIOS FOR THREE ELITES:
GEOGRAPHIC ORIGINS

Region	Business Leader	Federal Executive	Academic President
New England	1.43	1.14	1.04
Middle Atlantic	1.47	1.05	0.87
East North Central	1.18	0.95	1.04
West North Central	1.00	1.23	1.35
South Atlantic	0.57	1.00	0.93
East South Central	0.40	0.67	0.96
West South Central	0.44	0.67	0.97
Mountain	1.00	1.67	0.94
Pacific	1.33	1.00	0.81

TABLE 52
PROPORTIONAL REPRESENTATION RATIOS FOR THREE ELITES:
SIZE OF BIRTHPLACE

Size of Community	Business Leader	Federal Executive	Academic President
100,000 and over	2.06	1.71	0.92
25,000 to 100,000	1.71	1.50	1.60
2,500 to 25,000	1.57	1.40	1.19
Under 2,500	0.43	0.59	0.83

NOTE: For business leaders studied in 1952, the United States population distribution of the census of 1900 was used; for the 1959 federal executives, 1910, and for the 1968 academic presidents, the 1920 population.

academic presidents are more representative of the national population's residences as all ratios approach 1.00 rather closely. For business and government leaders, the distribution is skewed toward large urban areas.

Thus, the leaders represent all sizes of communities, although academic presidents are more likely to be from smaller communities than are business and government executives. In addition, the academic presidents are most nearly representative of the national population.

Family Influences

The heart of the analysis on family influences is based upon occupational mobility over three generations. It was found by Warner that there was a great percentage decrease from the grandfathers' to the fathers' generation insofar as farming as an occupational origin of business and government leaders is concerned. A similar pattern holds true for the grandfathers and fathers of academic presidents as shown in Table 53. Among all leaders, a very high percentage of grandfathers were farmers: 35 per cent of business leaders', 44 per cent of government leaders', and 43 per cent of academic presidents'. The grandfathers' sons moved to the cities to become major business executives, business owners, and professional men.

Higher Education Received

Warner found that higher education was the "royal road to success" for business and government leaders. About 57 per cent of

TABLE 53
THREE GENERATIONS OF OCCUPATIONAL MOBILITY

Occupation	Business Leaders		Government Leaders		Academic Leaders	
	Grandfather (per cent)	Father (per cent)	Grandfather (per cent)	Father (per cent)	Grandfather (per cent)	Father (per cent)
Farmer	35	9	44	14	43	16
Laborer	19	15	18	21	21	16
Owner of small business	17	18	14	14	11	11
Major executive and large business owner	12	31	6	17	3	10
Professional	10	14	10	19	15	31
Foreman	3	3	4	5	3	7
Clerk, salesman	2	8	3	9	1	5
Other	2	2	1	1	3	4
Total	100	100	100	100	100	100

business leaders and 81 per cent of federal executives were college graduates. In the academic president study it has been learned that all academic presidents are college graduates and nearly three-fourths have earned academic doctorates.

The list of institutions granting degrees to the three groups of leaders understandably contains similarities. Thus, the top five universities attended by business leaders were all Ivy League; in rank order they were Yale, Harvard, Princeton, Cornell, and Pennsylvania. For federal executives the top five were George Washington, Harvard, Columbia, Chicago, and Minnesota. Table 24 ranked the institutions granting doctorates (not the bachelor's degrees) for academic presidents and showed that the top five, which granted more than one-quarter of all presidents' doctorates, were Chicago, Columbia, Harvard, Catholic, and Yale.

Career Patterns

A scheme was used in a previous chapter showing the sequence of occupations in the presidents' career lines at five year intervals beginning with the first full-time job. Warner had developed similar patterns for business and government leaders and in Tables 54, 55, and 56 data are presented giving some selected broad pictures of such movements for all leaders.

TABLE 54
CAREER SEQUENCE OF BUSINESS LEADERS (1952)

Occupation	Beginning Occupation (per cent)	5 Years Later (per cent)	10 Years Later (per cent)	15 Years Later (per cent)
Laborer	14	3	1	0
Clerical, salesman	43	25	8	3
Minor executive	10	39	46	26
Major executive	1	6	26	57
Professions	24	21	14	10
Uniformed service	2	2	1	1
Business owner	1	2	3	3
Other occupations	5	2	1	0
Total per cent	100	100	100	100

The general pattern, as indicated in Table 54, was for business leaders to move through white-collar groups as all other occupational groups diminished. Although 14 per cent began as laborers, the percentage fell sharply after five years. There was also a fairly rapid movement out of the professions (mainly engineering and law) into business. Within fifteen years of becoming self-supporting, Warner found that more than one-half the men studied were major executives and another quarter were minor executives.

Forty-six per cent of the federal executives began their careers in the professions (mainly engineering, law, and education) and 25 per cent began as white-collar workers. As in the case of business lead-

TABLE 55
CAREER SEQUENCE OF FEDERAL EXECUTIVES (1959)

Executive's Occupation	Beginning Occupation (per cent)	5 Years Later (per cent)	10 Years Later (per cent)	15 Years Later (per cent)
Laborer	14	6	4	2
Clerical, salesman	25	17	8	3
Minor executive	5	17	28	26
Major executive	0*	2	7	21
Professions	46	46	45	42
Uniformed service	5	8	5	3
Business owner	1	1	1	1
Other occupations	4	3	2	2
Total per cent	100	100	100	100

*Less than 0.5 per cent.

ers, about 14 per cent began in laboring positions. Over the fifteen years there was little change among those in the professions, but those outside the professions moved into higher level executive positions. At the end of fifteen years, the three statuses of professional, major executive, and minor executive comprised 89 per cent of all federal executives. Over a few years, the men moved quickly out of laborer occupations as did the business leaders.

TABLE 56
CAREER SEQUENCE OF ACADEMIC PRESIDENTS (1968)

President's Occupation	Beginning Occupation (per cent)	5 Years Later (per cent)	10 Years Later (per cent)	15 Years Later (per cent)	20 Years Later (per cent)
Laborer	1	0	0	0	0
Clerical, salesman	2	1	0	0	0
Minor executive	1	1	0*	0*	0*
Major executive	1	1	1	1	1
Professions	90	90	94	95	96
Military	3	5	2	2	1
Business owner	0*	0*	0*	0*	1
Other occupations	2	2	3	2	1
Total per cent	100	100	100	100	100

*Less than 0.5 per cent.

The career sequence of academic presidents shows that over a twenty-year period, at least nine out of ten were in the professional fields—and, in education. It is significant that few presidents entered higher education outside of professional life. About one-third of the academic presidents began their careers as elementary-secondary teachers but just as quickly as business and government leaders left the laborer occupations, the future academic presidents left the elementary-secondary teacher positions and moved into principal, superintendent, and college faculty statuses. At the end of fifteen years, 30 per cent were presidents and at the end of twenty years, 63 per cent were presidents. There was a steady movement up the higher educational hierarchy from college teacher to department head to college dean or academic vice-president (provost) to president in the majority of cases.

On the basis of the career lines as presented in these tables, it is clear that: (1) much higher proportions of academic presidents (than of business or government leaders) were professionally trained, although a very high percentage of government leaders began in the professions; (2) much higher proportions of business leaders arose through laborer and white-collar occupations; and (3) higher proportions of business leaders reached major executive positions faster than did government leaders and faster than the academic leaders reached the presidency. It should be recalled however, that at the end of fifteen years, about 52 per cent of academic leaders were at high level administrative positions such as dean, vice-president or president—positions, comparable to many major business executive statuses.

In analyzing other aspects of business and government leaders' careers, Warner found that the average age of the civilian federal executives was 49.4 and the average age of business leaders was 53.7 years. In this research it was found that the average age of academic presidents is 52.9 years, or closer to that of the business leaders. It was also found that 45.3 years is the average age when business leaders assumed their present positions, while government executives were 44.8. In this study it was learned that the average academic president assumed his present position at the age of 45.1. Thus, the average age when business, government, and academic leaders assumed high levels of leadership in their respective hierarchies was around 45. Business and academic leaders had held their present positions for about eight years while federal executives were in their present positions about four years.

Among federal executives only 1 per cent are women, and among academic presidents, 11 per cent are women—10 per cent of whom are heads of Catholic liberal arts colleges for women and 1 per cent are heads of private liberal arts colleges for women. (No comparative figure for women was reported in the business leader study.) Although more women are found among academic presidents, they head liberal arts colleges for women, and no female president in the study heads a coeducational college or any university.

In conclusion, the comparative analysis of the three researches has built upon the perspective of the nature of modern society given so well by W. Lloyd Warner:

The American society is a fluid, emergent one, with change in the nature of the system. The local communities merge into a larger national collectivity. Large scale organizations, big government, and big business become increasingly prominent. In this fluid world of change and increasing immensity the managerial group will be drawn increasingly from the educated mobile men who come from the more populous lower occupational levels.[2]

It is clear that big education has a place among large scale organizations, and although a high percentage of academic presidents have professional origins, it is also evident that there are those from lower occupational levels represented. The men from lower level origins received a college education and advanced degrees and became active in the educational hierarchy as teachers and administrators leading to their current elite, academic administrative positions.

It was found that the occupational origins of academic presidents were quite similar to the other leaders in that their fathers were represented in disproportionately greater numbers in business executive, business ownership, and professional levels. And these high level positions were found among all three types of leaders in greater proportion than their representation in the adult, male United States population. However, there was evidence of mobility into the elites from relatively lower levels as well, especially from foreman and skilled laborer levels. Professional origins were especially prominent among all three elites, but among the academic presidents the professions most overrepresented were the clergy and elementary-secondary teaching, both of which were found in much greater proportions among the educators as opposed to the other leaders.

The business, government, and academic leaders came from all regions of the country, and although the southern states tended to produce fewer business and government leaders than other regions, the academic presidents were more representative of the national population's residence patterns. When the leaders' birthplaces were contrasted, it was found that while business and government leaders came primarily from large urban areas, the academic presidents were again more representative of the national population by coming from all sizes of communities in near proportions to the national average. However, the academic presidents were more apt to come from rural communities under 2,500 population or small towns when compared to the other two elites.

Research shows that among all leaders, a very large percentage of their grandfathers were farmers. In the case of business and govern-

2. W. Lloyd Warner, "Careers of American Business and Government Executives," p. 123.

ment leaders the grandfathers' sons tended to move to the large cities to become mainly business executives and business owners, and professional men. The rural to urban pattern held for academic presidents, but the movement was to small urban towns and predominantly to colleges to prepare for professional fields, especially teaching and the ministry.

While it was found that 57 per cent of the business leaders and 81 per cent of the government executives were college graduates—all academic presidents were college graduates and more than three-fourths had earned an academic doctorate. The leaders of all three elites showed great similarity in the universities attended as six universities were found among each group's top ten: Yale, Harvard, Michigan, New York, California at Berkeley, and Chicago.

When the career patterns of the elites were examined, it was found that much higher proportions of academic presidents were professionally trained, although a very high percentage of government leaders began their careers in professional fields. In addition, business leaders were more likely to rise through laborer and white-collar occupations than the others. It was also found that higher proportions of business leaders reached major executive positions faster than government leaders but not much faster than academic presidents' movements into high levels of administrative responsibility (dean or vice-president). The average leader assumed his present position at the age of 45.3 and was at the time of Warner's study, 53.7; the average federal executive assumed his present position at the age of 44.8 and was presently 49.4; the average academic president assumed his present position at the age of 45.1 and is now 52.9.

Relatively few women served as government executives or as academic presidents, although there were proportionally more women in higher education. But even in education, women headed liberal arts colleges for women (mainly Catholic), and no coeducational liberal arts college or university in the sample had a female president.

Research results indicated that although academic presidents came in greater proportions from higher occupational origins, the lower levels were also represented, as with business and government leaders. Society was found to be open and fluid so that persons of lower origins were able to make it to the top of all three hierarchies.

Suggestions For Future Research

At least five areas have been identified in this book as potentially fruitful for continued research that could build upon and extend the current knowledge of occupational mobility among elites in this society.

A study of the factors associated with the relative effectiveness of academic presidents of different institutions is needed.

The research in this study did not distinguish between the origins and career patterns of academic presidents based upon their relative effectiveness as chief administrators. Systematic research on those difficult and complex factors that make for more effective presidents and less effective presidents is crucial if the present unrest and excitement on campuses across the nation and the world are to be met by competent academic presidents. The problem of operationalizing some valid measure of presidential effectiveness is admittedly difficult, but it must be met openly and seriously by those interested in the future of higher education and this society. Careful and extensive research in this area could begin to identify those factors in one's career, background, style of leadership, philosophy of education, as well as the critical institutional factors that distinguish the most effective from the least effective academic presidents. Academic centers, research institutes, and development programs could create and use such information in the more effective preparation of academic presidents.

Necessary modifications of the Warner theory and methodology resulting in studies of occupational succession and careers of other groups in the society are needed.

The careers of physicians, lawyers, and ministers, other college administrators, professors, and labor union officials are only a few other occupational groups that could be studied to determine how real is the American Dream of open avenues to upward mobility. Studies of other elites could provide comparative bases that, like the present study, fill in the gaps of knowledge of occupational mobility in American society.

A similar study of the careers of America's two-year college presidents is needed.

Recognizing the dramatic growth and changes taking place in the multifarious junior and community colleges, attention could be focused on the careers of these two-year college presidents. The knowledge would be valuable in its own regard and would give a composite profile of the leaders in all of American higher education. It would also provide an important comparative analysis for the present study of the origins and careers of four-year college and university presidents.

A replication of the present study in ten years is needed.

The conclusions of the present research included the statement that this important hierarchy was neither closed nor rigid and persons of relatively lower social and occupational origins did make it into the elite of higher educational administration. However, just as W. Lloyd Warner benefitted from the Taussig and Joslyn study of business leaders in the 1920s (and he was able to use that study to determine if the society was becoming more or less rigid as seen through that occupation) so will the present research presumably offer a base-line to the study of academic presidents in 1980. In an era of swift change in the society and higher education, ten years would offer a reasonable comparative base.

Studies of the careers of key American Negroes and their occupational mobility in the society—how they moved into or were denied access to key positions—are needed.

Certainly, at this point in American history, when black and white Americans must face the question of equal opportunity more critically than ever before, knowledge of the careers of black Americans into elite positions is vital. Although racial aspects were not specifically delineated, there can be little question that the studies of business, government, and academic leaders have been basically of white men. Although those of lower level occupational origins have risen to the elites, the hypothesis offered is that very few were Negroes, and the career patterns have largely reflected white man's movement in the society. Identification of and research on the black man's occupational mobility will add an important element to whether American society is truly flexible to all its citizens, not only using occupational and geographical origins as indices, but also the color of a man's skin. Some Negroes hold that the avenues to elite positions are denied them as the educational and social systems continually work against them. The Warner theory and methodology could be modified to give factual evidence that brings clarity rather than emotion to this crucial social question.

It is hoped that this study has provided the reader with a greater sensitivity to the backgrounds of the men and women who are increasingly becoming the subject of much attention by the press, the legislature, the general public, as well as the campus community itself. For the most part, the men and women who head our institutions of higher education probably would concur with the views of the president who wrote the following:

> *There is no comparison whatsoever between the eases, joys, and peace of lesser positions and the frustrations and demands of the presidency. In theory, no one should accept the office—in practice, of course, thousands do.*

> *Would I do it again? Certainly. I can conceive more relaxed and perhaps blessed ways to live one's life, such as being a full professor in a great university, but life doesn't work that way. I agree with Carlyle that "our task is not to see what lies dimly in the future, but to do that which is immediately at hand."*

> *The academic presidency offers many of the challenges and satisfactions of administration in business and industry, the military or other fields, and yet, contains also the meaningful benefits of working with young people and watching them grow. It rewards with the thrill of victory by persuasion as in the field of politics, and the economic security and benefits of corporate administration. It gives one the feel that he is doing something important and it returns real dividends in social and professional status and prestige.*

There can be no question that in the next decade, the demands and frustration upon the academic president will be greater than ever before. Institutions will need those persons who can sense the action, the challenge, and the opportunity to give effective leadership to meet the needs of the publics within the academic community and to successfully interpret the institution's reasons for being to the larger society.

Appendix A

Research Design

There were no significant problems in universe definition and sample selection for the research in this study. The American Council on Education publishes selected data in its semi-annual directory of all accredited institutions of higher education in the United States.[1] The September 1967 issue of *Accredited Institutions of Higher Education* listed 1,259 such institutions along with the following information: (1) type of control (public or private, with religious affiliation, where appropriate); (2) type of institution (university, liberal arts college, teachers college, technological institution, military academy, junior college, seminary, professional school); (3) type and enrollment of students; (4) type of accreditation; and (5) name of the chief administrative officer.

After a careful review of the complete listing of institutions it was decided to exclude certain types of institutions that were accredited only as specialized professional schools not always possessing a base

---

1. American Council on Education, *Accredited Institutions of Higher Education* (Washington, D.C.: September, 1967). For a discussion on the meaning and use of accreditation, see pp. xiii–xv.

of liberal studies. It was believed that to include such four-year institutions might distort certain data about the career patterns, and since such institutions represented a very small fraction of students, faculty, and national resources, their omission for the purposes of this study would not be a serious limitation. With this in mind, the following four major categories of institutions were dropped at the outset: (1) private and public specialized professional schools, for example, art institutions, music academies, graduate schools for the professions such as foreign service or medical specialities; (2) private seminaries existing for the sole purpose of training persons for a particular religious order or denomination; (3) four-year institutions that have only been accredited as two-year programs by the respective accrediting (regional) association; and (4) multi-campus institutions presided over by the same administrative officer.[2] Some 141 colleges were identified as exempt; this left 1,118 institutions as the universe for the study. Table 1A gives a breakdown of the institutions of the academic presidents that composed the relevant population.[3]

The breakdown of institutions by geographical regions using the nine basic census regions (see Table 2A) was also useful in further defining the population. The relative sizes of the institutions given by student enrollments provided another important profile of the institutions of the presidents (see Table 3A).

2. For example, St. John's College of Maryland and St. John's College of New Mexico have the same president. To count both colleges in the study would be to duplicate the career data about the president and thereby distort the results. Only the major campus (or, in the St. John's case, the largest and oldest campus) was used in the regional analysis.

3. Colleges and universities are either public or private in the form of control. Virtually all *public* institutions are supported by the various states but a few depend primarily upon municipal or federal support. For *private* institutions, the colleges and universities are either supported by the Roman Catholic church, supported to varying extents by a Protestant religious organization or denomination, or the private institutions are *independent* and not supported to any important extent by a religious organization. In all cases, the notation that accompanied the formal accreditation was used to code institutions as either *public, Catholic, Protestant-related,* or *independent.*

All *technological institutions* have been kept separate in the analysis. This category also includes four military academies that have accredited engineering and technical programs.

The categorization of all institutions was based upon the instructions in this note, and it was followed throughout the book.

TABLE 1A

<small>DISTRIBUTION OF POPULATION OF THE STUDY</small>

Type of Institution		Number	Per cent
Public universities		134	12.0
Private universities		111	9.9
Catholic	(28)		
Protestant-related	(30)		
Independent	(53)		
Total universities		245	21.9
Public liberal arts colleges		232	20.7
Private liberal arts colleges		600	53.7
Catholic	(177)		
Protestant-related	(311)		
Independent	(112)		
Technological institutions		41	3.7
Total colleges		873	78.1
Total		1,118	100.0

TABLE 2A

<small>POPULATION BY GEOGRAPHICAL REGION</small>

Region of Institution	Number	Per cent
New England	100	8.9
Middle Atlantic	187	16.7
South Atlantic	174	15.6
East South Central	87	7.8
West South Central	98	8.8
East North Central	176	15.7
West North Central	141	12.6
Mountain	48	4.3
Pacific	107	9.6
Total	1,118	100.0

The presidents of all 1,118 selected four-year institutions were included in the research design itself, and thus the sample and the universe were identical. This method was adopted primarily to allow for enough responses from each type and size of institution throughout the nation so that comparisons, patterns, and analyses could be developed not only for the national sample but for different subdivisions of the whole.

TABLE 3A
POPULATION BY STUDENT ENROLLMENTS

Number of Students*	Number of Institutions	Per cent
Under 1,000 students	323	28.9
1,000 to 2,499	376	33.5
2,500 to 4,999	150	13.4
5,000 to 9,999	145	13.0
10,000 to 14,999	52	4.7
15,000 to 19,999	28	2.5
20,000 to 24,999	14	1.3
25,000 to 29,999	11	1.0
30,000 to 39,999	8	0.7
40,000 and above	11	1.0
Total	1,118	100.0

*Enrollment figures of each institution were taken from *Accredited Institutions of Higher Education,* 1967, and Table 3A was developed by classifying such figures as noted in the table.

Methods of Data Collection

Questionnaires served as the principal means of data collection about the presidents' careers. The research instrument developed by Warner for the business and government executives was modified to apply more directly to the college and university presidents; some items were kept virtually the same to allow for eventual comparisons among the elites. The questionnaire went through a series of changes, at each stage being subject to critical evaluation by a number of scholars in educational administration and social research.[4] Finally, there was a pilot test of the instrument with a sample of college presidents.

The questionnaire in its final form can be found in Appendix B. An open-ended item in the questionnaire answered by nearly 400 presidents asked why the respondent *chose* an educational career over any other career. It was aimed at exploring some of the stated and conscious motivations and values that the presidents perceived as playing roles in their career paths. A request was also made on the last page of the questionnaire for any speeches, reprints of arti-

4. Special thanks to Dr. Edward Blackman, Professor of Higher Education, and Dr. Dalton McFarland, Professor and Chairman of the Department of Management, Michigan State University, for their assistance and suggestions related to the development of the questionnaire.

cles, sources of books, or personal statements that outlined the president's philosophy of education and educational administration. Nearly 250 such statements of philosophy were sent by presidents of all types of colleges from all parts of the nation. Most respondents mentioned numerous problems, frustrations, and satisfactions that accompany the modern academic president's role.

Interviews

The studies of business and government executives made use of the Thematic Apperception Test in understanding the private worlds of these men, but no projective test was used in the academic president study. Nevertheless, personal interviews were conducted with a small number of college and university presidents. Some questions asked were elaborations of a few questionnaire items while the majority were developed to understand the respondent's views of his career, himself, and the world in which he operates. At the heart of the interviews was the problem of determining what motivates people to pursue careers in academic administration, that is, what values, ideologies, and situations lead them to their basic career patterns.

Supplementary Data

Selected reference works assisted in the collection of data regarding the president's type of college or university and the president's career. The *1967 College Blue Book* lists a variety of information about every college and university in the country, including: the president's name, the date of his inauguration, the degrees offered at the institution, faculty-student ratios, resources and endowments, annual income, and volumes in the library.[5] College catalogues and college guidebooks provided further valuable information about the institutions relevant to this study. All such data were coded and later arranged to give breadth to the understanding of the complexity and diversity in American higher education.

Since the majority of college presidents were included in the latest

5. *The 1967 College Blue Book* (New York: Yonkers-on-Hudson, 1967).

TABLE 4A
QUESTIONNAIRE RETURNS

Mailing	Number Mailed	Number Received	Per cent Received	Number Usable	Per cent Usable
Pilot	50	32	64.0	29	58.0
First	1,068	589	55.1	565	52.9
Second	497	188	37.8	166	33.4
Total		809	72.4	760	68.0

TABLE 5A
NON-USABLE QUESTIONNAIRES

Reasons Why Non-Usable	Number	Per cent
Respondent was acting or interim president	16	32.7
Respondent had no time to complete	9	18.4
Respondent had formal policy of not completing questionnaires	7	14.3
Respondent was either ill, recently resigned	3	6.1
Respondent was on leave, away from campus	2	4.1
Respondent headed military institution and felt most questions did not apply to his situation	1	2.0
Institution recently merged and person no longer was president	1	2.0
Completed questionnaires received after final deadline when data cards were placed in computer	10	20.4
Total	49	100.0

issue of *Who's Who in America (1968),* that volume served as a sourcebook for many facets of the president's life and career.[6]

Questionnaires were mailed to the 1,118 presidents of the selected American colleges and universities. Two mailings were used and a total of 809 questionnaires were received for a return of 72.4 per cent, of which 760 or 68.0 per cent were found usable. Table 4A gives the complete breakdown of the returns of the pilot study and the two major mailings. Table 5A shows that a total of forty-nine returned questionnaires were found non-usable and excluded from the study. In over one-half the non-usable cases, the presidents were either serving as acting or interim presidents or the completed questionnaires arrived after the final deadline when computer programming began.

6. *Who's Who in America,* 35 (Chicago: A. N. Marquis Company, 1968–69).

In the pilot study and the national mailings, analyses were conducted on samples of the non-respondents. There was no evidence that elements in the non-respondent's career pattern accounted for his refusing to answer the questionnaire.

Procedures for Data Analysis

The total sample included in the analysis consisted of the 760 questionnaires or 68.0 per cent of the universe. Subgroups of the 760 presidents were established both to check how representative the sample was of the universe and to provide meaningful subgroups to analyze the questionnaire items. Examination of these subgroups at this time will give a clearer understanding of the sample as well as the type of analysis used with the questionnaire responses. The first three subgroups presented below relate to the types of institutions the presidents represent, and the last three, to the presidents themselves.

The questionnaire responses of the presidents were contrasted by nine major classes as shown in Table 6A. By comparing Table 6A with Table 1A, one is able to determine the representativeness of the sample obtained. For example, 67.9 per cent of the nation's public university presidents are included in the sample of 760; 71.4 per cent of Catholic university presidents; 70 per cent of Protestant-related university presidents; 65.9 per cent of public liberal arts college presidents; 74 per cent of Catholic liberal arts college presi-

TABLE 6A
TYPES OF INSTITUTIONS REPRESENTED

Type of Institution	Number	Per cent
Public universities	91	13.0
Catholic universities	20	2.6
Protestant-related universities	21	2.8
Independent universities	29	3.8
Public liberal arts colleges	153	20.1
Catholic liberal arts colleges	131	17.2
Protestant-related liberal arts colleges	210	27.6
Independent liberal arts colleges	75	9.9
Technological institutions	30	3.9
Total	760	100.0

dents; 76.5 per cent of Protestant-related liberal arts college presidents; 67.0 per cent of independent liberal arts college presidents; and 73.2 per cent of the technological institution presidents. Thus, there is a proportional representation of public university presidents; a slight overrepresentation of presidents of Catholic and Protestant-related universities, Catholic liberal arts colleges, and technological institutions; and a slight underrepresentation of presidents of independent universities, public, Protestant-related, and independent liberal arts colleges. It is believed that the sample proves highly representative of the universe based upon the types of institutions of the presidents.

Contrasts of questionnaire data were made based upon the regional classifications of the colleges and universities to determine if geographical factors related to aspects of the academic presidents'

TABLE 7A

GEOGRAPHICAL LOCATIONS OF THE INSTITUTIONS

Region of Colleges and Universities	Number	Per cent
New England	63	8.3
Middle Atlantic	107	14.1
South Atlantic	103	13.6
East South Central	61	8.0
West South Central	62	8.2
East North Central	133	17.5
West North Central	117	15.4
Mountain	37	4.9
Pacific	77	10.1
Total	760	100.0

careers. By comparing Table 7A with Table 2A, one can assess the sample representativeness when considering the location of the institution. There is a very satisfactory representation for five regions, but the Middle Atlantic and South Atlantic states are slightly underrepresented in the sample (about 2 per cent), and the East North Central and West North Central states are slightly overrepresented by a similar percentage.

The study compared specific data about the presidents' careers based upon the relative sizes of their institutions using ten classes of student enrollments. This was done to determine if presidents of certain sizes of institutions had similar career patterns. Table 8A

TABLE 8A
STUDENT ENROLLMENTS OF THE INSTITUTIONS

Number of Students	Number of Institutions	Per cent
Under 1,000	214	28.2
1,000 to 2,499	260	34.1
2,500 to 4,999	102	13.4
5,000 to 9,999	98	12.9
10,000 to 14,999	41	5.4
15,000 to 19,999	16	2.1
20,000 to 24,999	8	1.1
25,000 to 29,999	9	1.2
30,000 to 39,999	5	0.7
40,000 and above	7	0.9
Total	760	100.0

shows the distribution of the sample using student enrollments.

The sample has an excellent proportional distribution for each class of institutional size in the population. A scanning of the per cent column in Table 8A with the per cent column of Table 3A shows the close parallel in institutional size in the universe and in the sample.

Sex of the Respondent

Specific analyses were made of the respondents' careers to determine if there were differences in the careers of women versus men.

TABLE 9A
DISTRIBUTION OF PRESIDENTS

Type of Institution	Males		Females		Total	
	Number	Per cent	Number	Per cent	Number	Per cent
Public universities	91	13.5	0	0.0	91	12.0
Catholic universities	20	3.0	0	0.0	20	2.6
Protestant-related universities	21	3.1	0	0.0	21	2.8
Independent universities	29	4.3	0	0.0	29	3.8
Public liberal arts	152	22.5	1	1.2	153	20.1
Catholic liberal arts	58	8.6	73	86.9	131	17.2
Protestant-related liberal arts	205	30.3	5	6.0	210	27.6
Independent liberal arts	70	10.4	5	6.0	75	9.9
Technological	30	4.4	0	0.0	30	3.9
Total	676	100.0	84	100.0	760	100.0

TABLE 10A
RESPONDENTS HAVING PREVIOUS POSITIONS AS PRESIDENTS

Type of Institution	Number Who Were Presidents of		
	One Other College	Two or More Other Colleges	No Other College
Public universities	16	6	69
Catholic universities	2	0	18
Protestant-related universities	2	2	17
Independent universities	4	2	23
Public liberal arts colleges	21	2	130
Catholic liberal arts	0	1	130
Protestant-related liberal arts	21	3	186
Independent liberal arts	7	0	68
Technological institutions	0	1	29
Total number	73	17	670
Per cent in each group	9.6	2.2	88.2

TABLE 11A
PRESIDENTS' TENURE IN PRESENT POSITIONS

Type of Institution	Number of Years in Present Position					
	Under One	1–4	5–10	11–15	16–20	Over 20
Public universities	8	32	32	9	7	3
Catholic universities	3	8	6	2	1	0
Protestant-related universities	0	7	5	1	2	6
Independent universities	5	11	10	2	1	0
Public liberal arts	8	54	42	24	16	9
Catholic liberal arts	15	49	41	15	7	4
Protestant-related liberal arts	15	69	61	31	20	14
Independent liberal arts	3	24	25	9	7	7
Technological institutions	4	9	11	2	1	3
Total number	61	263	233	95	62	46
Total per cent	8.0	34.6	30.7	12.5	8.2	6.1

TABLE 12A
OFFICIAL TITLE USED BY CHIEF ADMINISTRATOR

Title	Per cent
President	97.0
Chancellor	2.2
Rector	0.1
Superintendent	0.7
Total	100.0

TABLE 13A
NUMBER OF HONORARY DOCTORATES RECEIVED

	Number of Honorary Doctorates Received (Per Cent)							
Institution of President	*None*	*1*	*2*	*3*	*4–5*	*6–10*	*11–15*	*Over 15*	*Total Per cent*
Public university	37	18	10	10	12	7	4	2	100
Catholic university	74	0	6	5	5	5	5	0	100
Protestant university	15	30	10	15	15	10	5	0	100
Independent university	18	18	11	7	18	14	0	14	100
Public liberal arts	72	25	1	1	0	0	1	0	100
Catholic liberal arts	73	21	3	2	0	0	0	0	100
Protestant liberal arts	40	30	18	6	5	1	0	0	100
Independent liberal arts	36	33	11	6	8	4	1	0	100
Technological	44	28	8	4	8	4	0	4	100

In Table 9A, it can be seen that there were eighty-four women presidents included in the sample. All are associated with colleges rather than universities, and the vast majority of the females head Catholic colleges.

Table 10A gives an accurate distribution of the 12 per cent of college and university presidents who have presided over at least one other institution prior to assuming their present positions. A complete distribution by type of institution is given in Table 11A. In the actual tenure analysis of questionnaire items, the ninety presidents who had served as presidents of other institutions were excluded. Although a person might only have been in his present position three years, he might have held a prior presidency for fifteen years. To look upon him as being a relatively new college president would be an error and would affect the accuracy and meaning of the analysis by tenure.

Appendix B

Questionnaire

NATIONAL STUDY OF AMERICAN COLLEGE AND UNIVERSITY PRESIDENTS

1. What is your present age? . . . . ___(23-24)

   a) At what age did you first begin work as an educational administrator in a part-time capacity? _____ (25-26) and a full-time capacity? _____ (27-28)

2. What position-title do you now use in official correspondence?

   President . . . . ☐
   Chancellor . . . . ☐
   Provost . . . . ☐
   Rector . . . . ☐
   Superintendent . . . . ☐
   Other (Please specify)_____ ☐ (29)

3. At what age did you assume your present position? . . . . ___(30-31)

4. With how many colleges or universities have you been associated as a faculty member or an academic administrator (including your present institution)?

   One   Two   Three   Four   Five   Six   Seven   Eight and above
   ☐   ☐   ☐   ☐   ☐   ☐   ☐   ☐   (36)

5. Are you a member of one or more educational boards of trustees (or regents, directors) or high-level, policy-making committees in addition to your own institution?

   Please check one: Yes ☐   No ☐   (37)

167

a) Please identify the <u>NUMBER</u> of boards or policy-making committees on which you serve from the following types:

Type of Board	Number of Boards	
Your own institution's board	_____	(38)
Another college-university board	_____	(39)
Educational association	_____	(40)
Privately-supported foundation	_____	(41)
Publicly-supported foundation	_____	(42)
Business or industrial board	_____	(43)
Governmental commission or committee	_____	(44)
Other (Please specify)_____	_____	(45)

6. Are you . . . . . Male ☐   Female ☐ (50)   Married ☐   Spouse deceased ☐   Single ☐ (51)   Number of children _____ (52)

7. Have you been a president of a college or university at another institution(s) prior to assuming your present position?   Yes ☐   No ☐   (53)

   a) If so, please list the name of the institution and the date of your inauguration.

Name of College	Inaugural Date (year)
_____ (54-57)	_____ (66-67)
_____ (58-61)	_____
_____ (62-65)	_____

8. After beginning work on a full-time basis, what occupation did you engage in: (69-70)

Occupations	First Full-Time Position (71-72)	5 years later (73-74)	10 years later (75-76)	15 years later (77-78)	20 years later (79-80)
Educational					
Public school teacher	☐	☐	☐	☐	☐
Principal, superintendent . .	☐	☐	☐	☐	☐
Community college faculty . .	☐	☐	☐	☐	☐
Community college admin. . .	☐	☐	☐	☐	☐
College-university faculty. .	☐	☐	☐	☐	☐
Chairman of Department. . . .	☐	☐	☐	☐	☐
Dean of College	☐	☐	☐	☐	☐
College administrator below vice-president or second level in institution. . . .	☐	☐	☐	☐	☐
College administrator at vice-president or second level	☐	☐	☐	☐	☐
College president or chief administrative officer. . .	☐	☐	☐	☐	☐
Other (please specify)_____	☐	☐	☐	☐	☐
Other Professions					
Physician	☐	☐	☐	☐	☐
Lawyer.	☐	☐	☐	☐	☐
Clergy.	☐	☐	☐	☐	☐
Engineer.	☐	☐	☐	☐	☐
Other (specify)_____	☐	☐	☐	☐	☐
Business and Industry					
Worker--unskilled, semi-skilled	☐	☐	☐	☐	☐
Worker--skilled, mechanic . .	☐	☐	☐	☐	☐
Clerical worker, salesman . .	☐	☐	☐	☐	☐
Foreman, other minor executive	☐	☐	☐	☐	☐
Major business executive. . .	☐	☐	☐	☐	☐
Owner small-medium business (sales under $100,000). . . .	☐	☐	☐	☐	☐
Owner large business (sales over $100,000).	☐	☐	☐	☐	☐

Government Service
Local-state office holder . .
Federal elected office. . . .
Federal appointed office. . . .
Civil Service position. . . .
Other (specify)_____

Uniformed Military Service
Enlisted man or non-comm.off.
Commissioned Officer (please give
highest rank)_____

Farming or Ranching

9. Please give the following information about the position you held prior to assuming
your present position:
(6-7)   Title of position:_____
(8-9)   Name of institution, company, or organization:_____
(10-11)   Dates that you held that position: From_____to_____

10. If you were once a college teaching and/or research faculty member, please note at
the appropriate level the name of the institution at which you taught, the academic
department affiliation, and the years of the appointment: (15)

Faculty Rank	Name of Institution	Department	Dates
Lecturer			
Instructor			
Assistant Professor	18-21		
Associate Professor	22-25	34-35	36
Professor	26-29		37
	30-33		38

(39

11. Will you please fill in the following regarding your formal education at the
college level:

Institutions attended	Major Subject	Degree	Year Received Degree	Last Year Attended
40-43	56			
44-47	57			
48-51	58	(61-62)		
52-55	59-60			

12. Please check below any of the following to which you earned membership during
your undergraduate and graduate education:
Phi Beta Kappa ☐   (66)   Phi Kappa Phi ☐   (68)
Omicron Delta Kappa ☐ (67)   Other Honor Societies ☐_____
(69

13. Please list below the titles of books or articles published before or after becoming
a college president (including doctoral dissertation title, if applicable).
Please give dates of publication, if possible.

14. Have you been awarded an honorary degree from another college or university?
Yes ☐   No ☐   (70)

a) If so, please give the number of honorary doctorates received _____
and/or the number and types of other honorary degrees_____

15. Principal occupations of others in your family: (if deceased, please indicate previous occupation)

Occupations	Your Father when you began working full-time (71-72)	Your Father's Father (73-74)	Your Mother's Father (75-76)	Your Wife's Father (77-78)
Educational				
Public school teacher, administrator	□	□	□	□
Community college, faculty-admin. . .	□	□	□	□
College-university faculty	□	□	□	□
Chairman of Department.	□	□	□	□
College administrator below vice-president level	□	□	□	□
College administrator at vice-president level	□	□	□	□
College President	□	□	□	□
Other (specify)_____	□	□	□	□
Other Professions				
Physician	□	□	□	□
Lawyer.	□	□	□	□
Clergy.	□	□	□	□
Engineer.	□	□	□	□
Other (specify)_____	□	□	□	□
Business and Industry				
Worker, unskilled-semi-skilled. . .	□	□	□	□
Worker, skilled, mechanic	□	□	□	□
Clerical worker, salesman	□	□	□	□
Foreman, minor executive.	□	□	□	□
Major business executive.	□	□	□	□
Owner small-medium business (sales under $100,000)	□	□	□	□
Owner large business (sales over $100,000).	□	□	□	□
Government Service				
Local-state office holder	□	□	□	□
Federal elected office.	□	□	□	□
Federal appointed office.	□	□	□	□
Civil Service position.	□	□	□	□
Other (specify)_____	□	□	□	□
Uniformed Military Service	□	□	□	□
Farming or Ranching	□	□	□	□

(79-80)

16. Extent of schooling of your father and mother (please check only the highest category):

	Father (6)	Mother (7)
Less than high school . . .	□	□
Some high school.	□	□
High school graduate. . . .	□	□
Some college.	□	□
College graduate.	□	□
Post-graduate study	□	□

17. On the five-point scales below, please check that which you feel to be most relevant to the presidency of your institution, given the particular philosophy, needs, and goals of the institution as seen for the next ten years.

"Although the president must possess many administrative-leadership qualities, above all...

(8)   a)...the president must be a scholar in his own right with a notable background in teaching and research."

Extremely Important	Very Important		Not Very Important	Not Important At All

(9) b)...the president must be one who has demonstrated successful executive and
administrative abilities in educational administration."

Extremely	Very		Not Very	Not Important
Important	Important		Important	At All

(10) c)...the president must be one with considerable knowledge and training in business
or financial matters related to institutional growth and development."

Extremely	Very		Not Very	Not Important
Important	Important		Important	At All

(11) d) If you were asked to rank only the three major categories above as to the most
essential for the college president for your institution during the next ten years,
which would you place first (most crucial), second, third (least crucial).

Place 1, 2, 3 below

Teaching-Research Background . . . _____
Educational Administration Background_____
Business-Finance Background . . . _____

Please note any comments on special training and background that you feel
especially important for the college president that might not have been
covered in this section:

---

18. Please rank in order, from 1 to 7, the following functions in terms of the
percentage of time spent in each activity during a rather typical <u>month</u>
(1 is most time spent, 2 is next in time spent, etc.):

(15) _____ Educational activities and meetings at state and national levels
(16) _____ General administrative functions (including budget review, planning and
evaluating institutional affairs, policy meetings with central
administration or board, etc.)
(17) _____ Participation in and involvement with strictly fund-raising activities
for the institution
(18) _____ Conferences with faculty, students, alumni, and parents
(19) _____ Conferences with local, state, national government officials
(20) _____ Conferences with business and industrial leaders
(21) _____ Attendance at social occasions, community affairs, civic functions
Please give the approximate percentage of time you spend on the activities
you ranked Number 1 _____ and Number 2 _____

19. Of the time you spend with persons associated with the institution, please give the
approximate PERCENTAGE of time spent with each during a somewhat average week:

Approximate PER CENT
of Total Time

(24-25) _____ Board of Trustees members
(26-27) _____ Alumni
(28-29) _____ Students
(30-31) _____ Faculty members (on individual basis and with committees)
(32-33) _____ Administrative officers and staff of the institution
(34-35) _____ Civic, community leaders and committees
(36-37) _____ Other (please specify) _____

---

20. Place of Birth:

	Self (40)	Wife or Husband (41)	Father (42)	Father's Father (43)	Mother (44)	Mother's Father (45)
United States	☐	☐	☐	☐	☐	☐
Non-United States	☐	☐	☐	☐	☐	☐

21. What was the approximate population where your family lived at the time of your birth?

Rural or less than 2,500 ☐   Town of 2,500-10,000 ☐   City 10,000-15,000 ☐

City 15,000-100,000 ☐   City over 100,000 (or suburb) ☐   (46)

22. If American born, in which state? _____   (47-48)

23. From the time you completed your undergraduate education until the present, had you
     ever seriously considered a career outside the context of an educational institution?

                    Yes ☐   No ☐   (49)

     a) If so, please check the pertinent alternative(s) you have considered and
        CIRCLE the NUMBER of your <u>first</u> choice after a career in higher education: (50)
                                                                            (51)
              1. Business Executive . . . . . ☐   (52)
              2. Government Service . . . . . ☐
              3. Religious Service . . . . .   ☐
              4. Labor Union Official . . . . ☐
              5. Military Officer . . . . . . ☐
              6. Other (specify)_____   ☐
                                                                            (53)

ON THE BACK OF THIS PAGE (or any attached sheet) would you please tell us the reasons you
have chosen a career in administration in higher education as opposed to any other career.
(Write as much as you wish.)

We would find any comments you might have on any of the questions in this survey very
helpful. In addition, we would be most appreciative of any comments, sources and/or
reprints of articles and speeches in which you have given your philosophy of education
or academic administration related to the important role of your institution in American
higher education.

Bibliography

American College President and
American Higher Education

Blackman, Edward. Speech given at Michigan State University, College of Education, October 11, 1967.

Bolman, Frederick de W. *How College Presidents Are Chosen.* Washington, D.C.: American Council on Education, 1965.

Corson, John J. *Governance of Colleges and Universities.* New York: McGraw-Hill Book Company, Inc., 1960.

Demerath, Nicholas J., Stephens, Richard W., and Taylor, R. Robb. *Power, Presidents, and Professors.* New York: Basic Books, Inc., 1967.

Dodds, Harold W. *The Academic President: Educator or Caretaker?* New York: McGraw-Hill Book Company, Inc., 1962.

Hemphill, John K., and Walberg, Herbert. *An Empirical Study of College and University Presidents in the State of New York.* Princeton: Educational Testing Service, 1966.

Kerr, Clark. *The Uses of the University.* Cambridge, Massachusetts: Harvard University Press, 1963.

Prator, Ralph. *The College President.* Washington, D.C.: The Center for Applied Research in Education, Inc., 1963.

Rudolph, Frederick. *The American College and University: A History.* New York: Vintage Books, 1965.

Schmidt, George P. *The Liberal Arts College.* New Brunswick, New Jersey: Rutgers University Press, 1957.

Stoke, Harold W. *The American College President.* New York: Harper and Brothers, 1959.

Stroup, Herbert. *Bureaucracy in Higher Education.* New York: The Free Press, 1966.

Thwing, Charles F. *The College President.* New York: The MacMillan Company, 1926.

Wriston, Henry W. *Academic Procession.* New York: Columbia University Press, 1959.

Comparative Research on Business
and Government Executives

Warner, W. Lloyd. "The Careers of American Business and Government Executives: A Comparative Analysis." *Social Science Approaches to Business Behavior.* Edited by George B. Strother. Homewood, Illinois: Richard D. Irwin, Inc., 1962.

Warner, W. Lloyd, and Abegglen, James C. *Big Business Leaders in America.* New York: Harper and Brothers, 1955.

Warner, W. Lloyd, Van Riper, Paul P., Martin, Norman H. and Collins, Orvis F. *The American Federal Executive.* New Haven, Connecticut: Yale University Press, 1963.

Occupational Mobility

Rogoff, Natalie. *Recent Trends in Occupational Mobility.* Glencoe, Illinois: The Free Press, 1953.

Warner, W. Lloyd, and Abegglen, James C. *Occupational Mobility in American Business and Industry.* Minneapolis: University of Minnesota Press, 1955.

Occupational Selection

Faier, Bertram R. "Personality Factors in Occupational Choice." *Educational Psychological Measurement,* 13 (1953), 362.

Friedmann, E. A., and Havighurst, Robert J. "Work and Retirement." *Man, Work, and Society.* Edited by Sigmund Nosow and William H. Form. New York: Basic Books, Inc., 1962.

Ginzberg, Eli, Ginzberg, Sol, Axelrod, Sidney, and Herman, John. *Occupational Choice, An Approach to a General Theory.* New York: Columbia University Press, 1951.

Gross, Edward. *Work and Society.* New York: The Thomas Crowell Company, 1958.

Morse, Nancy C., and Weiss, R. S. "The Function and Meaning of Work and the Job." *Man, Work, and Society.* Edited by Nosow and Form, 1962.

Roe, Anne. *The Psychology of Occupations.* New York: John Wiley and Sons, Inc., 1956.

Super, Donald E. *The Psychology of Careers.* New York: Harper and Brothers, 1957.

Sample Definition and Selection

American Council on Education. *Accredited Institutions of Higher Education.* Washington, D.C.: American Council on Education, 1967.

U.S. Bureau of the Census, *Population, 1920.* Washington, D.C.: Government Printing Office, 1921.

U.S. Bureau of the Census, *Population, 1940.* Washington, D.C.: Government Printing Office, 1942.

Who's Who in America, 35 Chicago: The A. N. Marquis Company, 1968–69.